The Last Temptation of Zarathustra

Greg Fraser

> Was it not for you
> that the glacier's grey
> adorned itself today
> – with roses?

QUIDZUNC

ISBN 978-0-9775933-4-7

The Last Temptation of Zarathustra

∞

Greg Fraser

The Last Temptation of Zarathustra
Copyright Greg Fraser, 2009
All rights reserved

First published (private edition),
October, 2009

This reprint of the 2009 edition
published by QUIDZUNC,
August, 2024

National Library of Australia Cataloguing-in-Publication entry
Title: The last temptation of Zarathustra / editor, Greg Fraser.
ISBN: 9780977593347 (pbk.)
Subjects: Nietzsche, Friedrich Wilhelm, 1844-1900.
         Also sprach Zarathustra.
         Philosophy. Fiction in translation.
Other Contributors:
         Fraser, Greg.
Dewey Number: A822.04

Synopsis:
Faithful rendition of Nietzsche's *Also Sprach Zarathustra*, *Part IV*, in English playscript adaptation. Includes stage directions and original German text in a beautiful Fraktur font.

Contents

Dedication 7
Dramatis Personae 9
Synopsis 11
Prologue 15
Act One 16
    The Honey Sacrifice 16
    The Cry of Distress 19
    Conversation with the Kings 21
    The Bloodsucker 25
    The Enchanter 28
    Out of Service 33
    The Ugliest Man 37
    The Voluntary Beggar 40
    The Shadow 43
    N o o n 46
Act Two 50
    The Homecoming 50
    The Late Supper 54
    Zarathustra's Symposium 56
    Of the Higher Man 58
    The Symphony of Flatulence 64
    The Song of Melancholy 65
    On Science 69
    Among the Daughters of the Wilderness 72
    The Awakening 77
    Assover 80
    The Song of Intoxication 83
    The Sign 90
Zwischenspiel 95
Also Sprach Zarathustra 97

Dedication

The *Last Temptation of Zarathustra* is first and foremost *a play*. It has been written to be played. It has not been my intention to merely rework the genius of Nietzsche's original, here, into yet another pallid and stilted translation, though in a new form. Rather I have sought to show just how much can be gained by a little idiom, freedom, and "theatrical interpretation." It is in this spirit that I present this playscript to the eyes of the public –
– Zarathustra and his contagonists are wonderful characters. They deserve a good playing. To that end, this book needs a readership that can give this play a public. Creative readers. Actors & Artists. Doers. Thus I dedicate this book – and this play, – *not* to the studious preservers of things past, but to the active creators of things to come: *to those who can act.*

Greg Fraser,
February 2009

Dramatis Personae

Zarathustra — a retired sage. Groucho Marx as Friedrich Nietzsche.

The Old Prophet — alias "The Prophet of the Great Weariness." Carries, and is weighed down by his own soap box.

The Kings to Right and Left — Twins. Shades of Tweedledum and Tweedledee.

The Conscientious of Spirit — a scientist. Looks like Albert Einstein.

The Enchanter — a man of the Theatre. Mel Gibson as Richard Wagner.

The Old Pope — an undertaker. Retired due to lack of work. Abraham Lincoln with eye-patch.

The Ugliest Man — aka "The Murderer of God." An atheist. Phyllis Diller with cigar?

The Voluntary Beggar — a philanthropist. Looks like Ghandi.

The Shadow — Zarathustra's shadow. A waiflike orphan. Possibly female.

A Mule

Chorus of Satyrs & Maenads — **Zarathustra's Soul,** a prima ballerina; **The Daughters of the Wilderness,** a chorus of belly-dancers;
— **Zarathustra's Pets:** an Eagle, a Serpent, a Lion, Doves, etc.

Synopsis

Zarathustra has retired from his travels as itinerant sage, to a mountaintop, where he wallows in his own happiness and awaits the advent of his true disciples. One morning, however, the Old Prophet of Doom appears and announces the coming of a Great Cry of Distress, to which, he foretells, even Zarathustra – the last happy man – must eventually succumb.

Hearing the cry himself, Zarathustra runs out from his cave in search of the afflicted soul, whom he imagines to be beset by some mortal danger in the wilds nearby. In so doing, he meets a whole series of unlikely, but archetypal characters – the Kings to Right and Left, the Old Enchanter, the Retired Pope, The Ugliest Man, the Conscientious of Spirit, the Voluntary Beggar, and even an old immoralist who claims to be his Shadow – from whom he eventually finds himself running away – but not before inviting each in turn to share the security and sanctuary of his own cave for the coming night.

On his way home Zarathustra stops and rests, beguiled by the most perfect Noontide – in which he becomes lost between the reflections of his own soul and those of the heavens above. Returning to himself and – later that evening – to his own cave, Zarathustra is greeted by a chorus of the so-called "Higher Men" – those whom he has invited to be his guests during the morning of the now-dying day. Unable to distinguish between their chorus and the prophesied Great Cry of Distress, Zarathustra settles to the task of host.

The evening becomes a riotous symposium – covering the topics of Science, Sensuality, and the Higher Man – and culminating in a realization by each of the guests, that he has, each in his own way, come through Zarathustra to a newfound vigour, and health: a convalescence signalled – much to Zarathustra's disgust – by their worshipful celebration of an Ass-fest in the very moment when he had ducked out of the cave for a little fresh air and "relief from the stuffiness of the Higher Men."

One by one, however, they join him in the moonlight, where the Ugliest Man – a.k.a. "The Murderer of God" – pronounces her willingness to live her entire, hitherto meaningless life over again, all for the sake of this one day, all for the sake of even just one evening with Zarathustra. Just then, the midnight bell tolls in the distance, and the day ends in an ecstatic chorus of maenads, satyrs, and newly-invigorated Higher Men.

When Zarathustra wakes next day, however, to bask once more in his place in the sun, he finds his house-guests all still huddled in the shadows of the cave. That these Higher Men are not those for whom he has waited – not his true disciples – is illustrated by the coming of new animals to the assembly of Zarathustra's house pets: a flock of doves, and a lion – from which the emergent Higher Men all flee in fear: leaving one last great Cry of Distress ringing in the ears of their now transformed onetime host.

End

The Last Temptation
of Zarathustra

A festival-play

Zarathustra's Prologue

Exterior. Zarathustra's Cave. Dawn.

Chorus of satyrs and maenads lie sleeping in a ring about a large, flat boulder before the cave.

Zarathustra (*steps from the cave to greet the sunrise*): O Great Star! What would thy happiness be if thou hadst not those for whom thou shinest?

Ballet ensues, in which satyrs and maenads dance a rather formal "Celebration of Life". Zarathustra makes his way to the boulder, then sits.

Act One

1 – Exterior. Zarathustra's Cave. Early Morning.

Zarathustra, in lotus position, basking on the boulder, looks out over valleys and mountaintops.

Chorus (*dance sprightly, but in measured steps about the boulder, and sing as in a roundelay*): O Zarathustra – On the lookout for your happiness?
Zarathustra (*sings*): Happiness? What lies in happiness? It's been a long time since I strove for happiness. I strive now in my work!
Chorus: O Zarathustra, you say that like someone who has more than enough of everything good. Do you not wallow in a sea of happiness as blue as the oceans themselves?
Zarathustra: You scamps, you scallywags, how well you chose the likeness! But you know it too, my happiness is heavy and nothing like a flowing fountain. It sticks to me and won't come off. It hangs 'round like a bad smell.
Chorus (*repeat his words as if trying to fathom them, then sit all around*): O Zarathustra, that's how you come to be getting ever browner and browner. You've become darker indeed, though your hair does seem to be going white. Lo and behold, you're sitting in a mess of your own making!
Zarathustra (*Jumping up to check his backside, then laughing*): What's that, my pets! Truly I made a muck of it when I spoke of bad smells. But what's happened to me is what happens to every fruit that ripens. It's the honey in my veins. It makes my blood thicker, and my soul more peaceful too.
Chorus: So it shall be, O Zarathustra. But are you going, today, to climb some high mountain? The air is clear, and one sees more of the world, today, than ever before.
Zarathustra: Yes, my animals one-and-all, that's splendid advice, and after my own heart. I will climb some high mountain today! But take care that there be honey on-hand up there. Golden, clear, honeycomb- and daisy-fresh honey. For you know, there above, I shall make the Honey Sacrifice!

Ballet ensues, in which Zarathustra makes his way to a higher plateau, accompanied by a few Maenads, whom he ultimately sends home.

2 – Exterior. Mountain Plateau. Early Morning

Zarathustra laughs, and dances throughout the following with stock in hand. Zarathustra's Soul is seen lurking in the shadows of various boulders.

Zarathustra: That I spoke of sacrifices and offerings of honey – it was merely a twist-and-turn of phrase, and verily, a necessary folly! Here on high I can speak more freely than in front of hermit's houses and hermit's housepets. What sacrifice? I squander the cards I'm dealt – a prodigal with a thousand cards-to-play – how should I call that a sacrifice! And as I longed for honey, I was longing only for the bait – the sap and syrup that baits the breath of grizzly bears and grumble-bums – for the best of bait, gobsmacking stuff, fit for a hunter- and fisher-of-men. For, though all the world be darkest jungle, and all the wilds be hunter's playgrounds, to me they are sooner and better abundant bottomless seas – seas full of colourful fish, and crabs, all of a sort to tantalize and tempt a god to play, and to fish and cast his nets – so rich is the world in wonders great-and-small! Especially the world-of-men, the human sea – for whom I cast my golden fish-hook out and speak: Heave yourself up, you abyss of humanity! Heave yourself up and hurl your fish and most glittering crabs to me! With my best bait I lure today the most wonderful human fish! My happiness itself I cast out far and wide, between the rising and the noon-tide – and the going-down: in case a few human fish learn to latch-onto and catch-onto my happiness. Until they – biting on the barbs of my hidden snares – have no choice but to rise up to my level: from the bottom of the abyss, the most motley – up to the most malicious, mischievous fisher-of-men. That's who I am, precisely, from the ground up, and foremost: a draughtsman (*draws with his stock*), a drawer (*pulls on his stock*), a dragger (*drags a toe*), a dragoon (*slams the point of the stock down*), a dancer and dancemaster, a head (*as if aside:*) – and toe – master: one who wasted no breath when he said "Become who you are!" (*slams the stock again*) Thus, now, humanity must come up here to me, for I still await the sign that it is time for me to go down. I cannot allow my sun to set until I have gone amongst men. Thus I wait here, shrewd and haughty, high in the mountains, neither impatient nor patient, much more as one who has unlearned patience altogether – nothing under sufferance, I suffer no more. My fate, to be exact, leaves me time for everything. Unhurried. Unworried. Perhaps Fate has even forgotten me altogether? Or does she sit behind some great stone, in the shadows, catching flies? And truly, I am grateful to my eternal fate, that she does not hurry or hound me, that she leaves me time for pranks and mischief, for the purpose of which, today, I have climbed to this lofty peak. Has a man ever caught fish so high in the mountains? And even if it is a piece of folly to wish for – let alone to fish for such things – better yet folly than that I stay low, dwelling down there on such things, turning green, then gold, a prized mouldy old bellows of expectation (*coughs phlegmatically, as if to spit*) a thundering storm of self-righteousness, sweeping out of the mountains, impatient, dogmatic, unleashed and howling through the valleys "Hear me, or I shall lash you all with the scourge of God!" Not that I should be upset at such tempers. I think them good for a laugh. How impatient these bugle-blowers must be, who trump it up "now or never!" But me and my fate, we speak to neither this day, nor the next, nor to never. We have time on our hands for talking, time and time again. For it must come to pass at least once. (*traces circles, like a torus, in the soil with his toes and cane as he dances and sings*) There's no way to by-pass that which must come. There's no side-stepping what must come to pass: our great Hazara! our great far-off kingdom-of-man, a Zarathustra-time of a thousand years. How far off can far-off be? Is that my concern! But for all that it stands no less certain to me. With both feet I stand sure on this ground, on an eternal footing, on the hardest bedrock; on this monolithic, megalithic, prehistoric, panoramic mountaintop – to which the four winds come as to watersheds, asking Where? And Whither? And Whence? – What mischief and malice moves me to laughter in this! Pure laughter! Sacred laughter! Throw down thy glittering, taunting laughter, O Malice, from the mountaintops! Bait me up the most beautiful fish of mankind with thy gleam! And that which in all of the oceans belongs to me, my in-and-for-myself in all things: fish that up to me! Lure and lead that up to me here! That's why I wait. Me, the most malicious of all fisherfolk. Out you go! Out you go, my hook! Downwards, inwards, bait of my happiness! Drizzle thy sweetest dew, o honey-sweet blood of my heart! Bite, Hook, in the belly of all melancholy! (*sits on a boulder*) Out you go! Out you go, too, my eye! Oh how many seas surround me here! What waxing and waning futures of men! And above me – what a rosy-red calm! What a clearing – of silence.

Zarathustra has begun to trace the outline of his own shadow on the ground with the tip of his cane, but jumps up with a start and a little squeal as he sees the shadow of another appear beside his own.

3 – Exterior. Mountain Plateau. Morning

Zarathustra turns to see the Old Prophet. The two stand motionless studying each other's faces, while the Chorus dance around them. The Old Prophet's face is illuminated.

Chorus (*sing a roundelay*): Nothing really matters! Nothing is worthwhile! The world has no rhyme nor reason! Nothing but nausea comes of knowledge!

The roundelay ends as the Old Prophet passes his hand before his face, as if to wash away its history. Zarathustra does the same. They breathe deeply, as if refreshed by the ritual, then shake hands.

Zarathustra: Be thou welcome, O Prophet of the Great Weariness! You shall not have once been my board-and-bedfellow in vain. Eat and drink with me today, too, and forgive it me that a happy old man sits with you at the table!

Old Prophet: A happy old man? Whoever you are – or think you are – O Zarathustra, your time on this high has nearly caught you up. Your backside shall soon get a good wetting!

Zarathustra: Am I, then, all washed up? (*as if aside:*) Leastways this is not sizing up to be a dry argument!

Old Prophet: The waves around thy mountaintop are welling up, O Zarathustra. The waves of great anguish and distress: they shall soon lift the seat off thy pants, too, and carry them off. Haven't you heard? Has it not raged and roared its way here from the very depths?

Zarathustra listens. Motif in the orchestra here, and at other critical places, representing "The Great Cry of Distress."

Zarathustra: You bringer of bad tides: that's a cry of distress, and a human one too. Well it may come out of some sea of troubles. But

what have I to do with the tribulations of humanity! My final sin, reserved for me still, do you know what it is?
Old Prophet: Pity! O Zarathustra. I have come to tempt you on to your final sin! Do you hear it? Do you hear, O Zarathustra? The cry is for you! It beckons unto thee: "Come! Come! Come! It is time. It is highest time!"

Zarathustra's Soul is seen in the background, wearing a bride's veil, and pirouetting across the scene.

Zarathustra: And who is it, then, that calls for me so?
Old Prophet: But you know well already. Why hide thyself? It is the Higher Man. The Higher Man it is – and crying out for you.
Zarathustra (*alarmed*): The Higher Man? What does he want? Him? The Higher Man! What does he want here?
Old Prophet (gloomily): O Zarathustra, there you stand, and not like one who jumps for joy. You are beside yourself, and need now to be quick on your feet, I'd say, lest you fall apart. But even if you choose to dance here before me, and all thy cartwheels turn, no one could yet say to me: "Behold! Here dances the last happy man!" Seeking *him* one should come to this giddy height in vain. Caves he should find, and caverns, hideouts for hideaways, but not goldmines and treasure-chests and motherloads of happiness. Happiness – how should one find happiness among cave-dwellers and hermits! Must I seek the ultimate happiness still on islands of blessedness, in far off and forgotten seas? But it's all the same, it doesn't pay, it's no use searching, there are no islands of blessedness anymore!
Zarathustra: No! No! Thrice no! I know better than that! There are still islands of blessedness! Go quietly thereabouts, you sighing sack of sadness! Sputter no more about it, you mid-morning raincloud. Do I not stand here already, wet from your misery, and soaked like a dog? Now, to get dry, I shall shake myself and run free: you shouldn't wonder at it! Do you think me unmannerly? Ah, but I am lord of this manor! (*breathes deeply of the beautiful vista before them*) And as for your Higher Man? Well then! I shall seek him out in the woods straightaway: thence came his cry. Perhaps some wild beast is pressing hard upon him. But he is in my domain, and herein he shall come to no harm! (*aside:*) And truly, there is many a terrible beast here about me.
Old Prophet: O Zarathustra, you are a scoundrel. I know it well: you want to be free of me! Sooner still you run off into the woods and

stalk wild beasts. But what will it help you? Come evening thou shalt have me again: in thine own cave I shall sit, tired, like a log, and tight – in wait for thee!
Zarathustra: So be it! And what is mine, my friend, in my cave, belongs also unto you: be my guest! And should you find honey there, well then! Lap it up, you old grizzly, and sweeten your soul a little! For, come evening we shall both be good things – and glad – good things and glad that this day should have run its course! And you yourself shall dance to my tunes. I shall sing and you shall be my dancebear. You don't believe it? You shake your head? Well then! Up now, Old Bear! For you shall see that I too – am a prophet (*runs off*).

4 – Exterior. Somewhere in the mountains. Morning

Zarathustra bounds through the woods, but stops dead in his tracks when he sees the Kings to Right and Left, replete with crowns and purple robes, leading a fully-laden mule.

Zarathustra: What do these kings want in my domain? (*hides himself*) Strange. Strange. Is this a rhyme for a fool? Two kings I see – but only one mule!

Right and Left look at each other as if their own thoughts had just been spoken aloud.

Right: Why, we're of the exact same opinion ...
Left: ... just quietly.
Right: Yes, one simply doesn't say such things out loud.
Left: It must have been a goatherd.
Right: Or a hermit.
Left: Well then, he's lived too long with no-one but rocks and trees. Lack of good company, you know: It ruins the manners.
Right: Good company? From whom, then, are we on the hoof? Is it not from "Good Company"? Good Manners – better, really, to live among goatherds and hermits, than to have no-one but our gilded, false, overpowdered rabble in train – even if they do call themselves "Good Company". Even if they do call themselves "the cream of the

crop". Everything about them is false and foul, not least their blood.
You can thank that on some nasty old diseases. (*grabs his crotch*)
Left: And some nastier old physicians! (*grabs his crotch*)
Right: The cream, nowadays, is really a good, healthy farmboy: gruff, clever, toughskinned, stubborn: that, really is the best you can get. The farmer is best, and farm-types should rule! Instead we have the rabble and rule of the mob – my delusions are gone. The mob is a hotch-potch. Riff-raff. Hickelty-pickelty. Saint and Sinner. Hero, Harlot, Highbrow, Lowbrow, great and small – and whatever else could make its way out of the ark. Good manners! With us it's all false and foul. No one knows any reverence anymore: that's what we're fleeing. The fawning, drooling dogs: even their laurels are gilt-over. (*whirls his crown around on his finger*) I'm choking with disgust to think that even we kings have become false: draped over and hidden behind the yellowing old glories of our grandfathers: showpieces for every horse-trading fool who dreams of power – or wakes for a game of chess! We're not the first and foremost: yet that's what we stand for: well, we're sick and tired of it, we're not going to stand for such sleight-of-hand anymore. We're on the run from the whole pushy, trouble-making, scandal-mongering, fish-mongering, rabble-rousing mob ... whose breath – phew! To live with such riff-raff – phew! To be first among the rabble! Oh (*vomits*) phew! What is it befits us kings anymore!
Left: Your old disease has struck you again, O brother of mine. It's wretched. The old nausea is back. And you know, while we're at it, we have an audience.
Zarathustra (*coming out*): Your audience, my Kings, your gleeful audience-of-one, is none other than Zarathustra. I am he. Zarathustra, who once was heard to say "What is it befits a king anymore!" Forgive me, but I rejoiced in my heart when you said to each other "What befits us kings?" For this is my domain and my kingdom: What on Earth could you be after here in my domain? Perhaps, rather, you have found something in your travels that I am after: namely, the Higher Man.
Right and **Left:** We are discovered!
Right (*drawing a sword and duelling an imaginary foe*): With the edge of these words you have hacked away the thickest blackness ... (*seems lost for words*)
Left: ... of our hearts.
Right: You have exposed ...

Left: ... our distress.
Right: For behold! We are underway precisely ...
Right and Left: ... in search of the Higher Man!
Right: The one above us ...
Left: ... though we be kings.
Right: To him we are taking this mule.
Left: The Highest Man, precisely ...
Right: (*interrupting*) ... shall be the mightiest ruler on Earth.
Left: There is no more savage misfortune in all human history ...
Right: ... than that the most powerful on Earth ...
Left: ... are not also ...
Right and Left: ... the first among men.
Right: That's how it comes that everything is false ...
Left: ... and crooked ...
Right: ... and monstrous.
Left: And when they are properly the last ...
Right: ... and least fit to rule ...
Left: ... and more like sheep ...
Right: ... than men ...
Left: ... the value of the rabble ...
Right: ... climbs and climbs ...
Left: ... until ...
Right: ... finally ...
Left: (*speaking very fast, to avoid interruption*) ... the virtue of the mob itself ...
Right: ... speaks.
Right and Left: "Behold! I alone am virtue!"
Zarathustra: What's this I hear? Wisdom from the mouths of kings! I am uplifted, and, truly, moved to make a song about it all – though it be a rather unpopular tune, and not at all fit for everyday consumption. (*as if aside, and only incidentally patting the mule*) I have long unlearned all consideration for those with overlong ears. Well then! Here goes! (*sings*) Once –
Mule (*interrupting, as if with deliberate sarcasm*): Ye-ah!
Zarathustra: ... in the very first year of man's redemption –
　　　　　The Sybil uttered this drunken contention:
　　　　　"Now things are bad, oh Woe!
　　　　　Decline? Never sank the world so low!
　　　　　Rome's sunk to whoredom, a brothel too,
　　　　　Caesar's a cow, and God – a Jew!"

There is a long pause
Right: O Zarathustra, what a gambit! How lucky for us ...
Left: ... that we gambled on seeing you.
Right: Your enemies, you see, showed us your image ...
Left: ... in their mirrors.
Right: You looked so scornful and haughty ...
Left: ... with the scowl of a devil ...
Right: ... that we were afraid of you. (*looks at Left, waiting for another interruption*) But what could we help it! (*looks again*) Ever and anon you pricked our ears ...
Left: ... and needled our hearts ...
Right: ... with your sayings... Finally we said ...
Right and **Left:** "What does it matter how he looks!"
Right: We had to lend an ear to him who taught ...
Left: "You shall love peace as a means to new wars, and the short peace more than the long!"
Right (*annoyed at the continual interruptions*): No one ever spoke such warlike words ...
Left: "What is good?"
Right (*poking Left with his finger, as if with a sword*): "It is good to be brave!"
Left (*stabbing back at Right in similar fashion*): "It is the good war that hallows every cause."
Right: O Zarathustra, the blood of our fathers raged in our breasts at such words. (*pushes Left like a schoolboy, trying to hide the mischief from Zarathustra*) It was like the mention of Springtime to old winebarrels.
Left (*returns the push in similar fashion*): When swords crossed each other like red-speckled snakeskins, life ...
Right (*poking Left, as before*): ... to our fathers ...
Left (*poking Right*): ... was a good thing. How they would sigh ...
Right (*poking, as before*): ... our fathers ...
Left (*pushing Right away flagrantly, with both hands*): ... if they saw dull edgeless swords on the wall!
Right: Like them, they thirsted for action (*boxes left, very clumsily, across the ear*)
Left: Swords, you see, simply live for the taste of blood. (*hits back with even less poise*)

An undignified scuffle ensues, but ends quickly, as neither Right nor Left are at all capable of hostilities.

Zarathustra (*makes a face, aside, then motions with his hand*): Well then! That's the way! There lies the cave of Zarathustra! (*aside:*) – And this day shall have a long evening indeed! – But for now, a cry of distress calls me urgently away. It would honour my cave, however, if kings should choose to sit there in waiting. (*aside:*) – Though, honestly, it'll soon be standing-room only! –

Zarathustra watches the kings as they run inelegantly out of sight, chasing the mule, who seems to be leading the way.

Zarathustra: Still, what's to be done about it! Are castles and courtrooms really not the best places on Earth for a good grounding in – standing around? And the sole remaining virtue of kings: does it not simply boil down, nowadays, to being last – in a very long line?

Right and Left go out of sight. Zarathustra heads off in the opposite direction.

5 – Exterior. Swamp. Morning

Zarathustra, dancing sprightly, picks his way through some very swampy ground. Unwittingly, he steps on the Conscientious of Spirit, who is lying prostrate with his arm in the mire.

Conscientious of Spirit (*cries out in pain*): Argh! Jesus Christ!

Zarathustra is so surprised that he reflexively takes to the squirming figure with his cane.

Conscientious of Spirit (*yells a profanity as each blow lands*): Shit! Christ! Fuck! Jesus! Shit! Shit!

Zarathustra realizes there's no danger, and helps the victim up, bemused.

Zarathustra (*kneeling*): Forgive me!
Conscientious of Spirit (*sitting*): Holy Hell! Shit!

Zarathustra (*squatting comfortably, on one knee*): Forgive me, and let me set you straight, now – with a parable: Like a wanderer roaming a lonely road, dreaming of distant things, looking out – but not for a sleeping dog (*aside:*) – A sleeping dog lying – lying in the sun: I run into you; we have a run in; will we fight to the death? No, frightened to death, we fought, but how little had failed that they had simply found each other, this loner and this dog, playfully, kindly, in kind – for are they not two of a kind? namely: alone!
Conscientious of Spirit: See here you, whoever you are – or think you are – you have overstepped the mark with your parable, and not just with your foot! Am I a dog then, that you can walk all over me like this?

Zarathustra notices several trickles of blood on the other's forearm.

Zarathustra: But what are you up to down there, you poor devil. What has cut you so deep? Have you been bitten by some unholy beast?
Conscientious of Spirit (*laughs*): What concern is that of yours? I am at home here in my domain. Question me who will, I shall answer a goose with a gander.
Zarathustra: You're on the wrong track, my friend. This is not your six feet of earth at all, this is my domain, and here no one shall come to grief! Call me what you will, I am who I must needs be (*jumps to his feet*) Well then! I call myself Zarathustra. Up that way is the path to my cave: it isn't far – won't you lick your wounds with Zarathustra? It goes badly for you, poor devil, in this life: first you were bitten-over by beasts, and then trodden-under by man.
Conscientious of Spirit (*lays back on the ground, outstretched, as if transformed, in a sort of reverie*): But what has happened to me! Who else has cared for me in this life, but this one man, namely Zarathustra, and that one beast, namely the bloodsucker – the leech? For the sake of the leech I lay here in this swamp, like an angler; and my arm had been bitten-over ten times already, when an even greater blood-sucker happened to strike – Zarathustra himself! What luck! What a wonder! Praised be the day that lured me into this swamp! Praised be the best blood-pumping brain-drainer alive today: praised be the great leech-of-conscience himself: Zarathustra!
Zarathustra (*heartily reaching out his hand, and pulling the other to his feet*): Who are you? There's a lot to be cleared-up and cheered-up between us: but already, I think, it's a fine, clear day.

Conscientious of Spirit: I am The Conscientious of Spirit, and no one could take matters of conscience firmer, faster, nor harder than I – except for Zarathustra himself, from whom I learnt them. Better to know nothing, than to half-know everything! Better a naked fool, than a dressed-up sage in borrowed robes! These are grounds to go by: What does it matter if they be great or small? whether called Swamp or Sky, Heaven or Earth? An arm's length of ground is good enough, so long as it's Good Grounds, and sound! An arm's length of ground: one can stand firm upon it. In the exact science of conscience, you know, there is nothing large and nothing small.
Zarathustra: So you know leeches from the ground up? And you've followed the leech down till you found Common Ground: How conscientious!
Conscientious of Spirit: O Zarathustra, that would be a monstrous undertaking. How could I even consider it? But that of which I am knowledgeable, and truly master, is the leeches brain – that is my world! Forgive my pride, O Zarathustra, speaking up for me in this, but here I am without equal. Thus did I say "This is my home". How long have I pursued this one thing – the brain of the leech – that the slippery truth not slip past me here! Here is my domain! For this I threw all else away; for this every other thing came to be all-the-same to me, and equal; so that hard by my glowing knowledge is the pitch of my ignorance. It's black. In matters of the spirit, my conscience demands of me that I know one thing only, and all-things-else not-at-all. I am sickened by allhalf-measures of spirit, by everything hazy and hovering and half-blown. Where my honesty ends, I am blind – and wish to be blind, what's more. Where I wish to be in-the-know (*taps the side of his nose*), there I demand no self-deception, just honesty: firm, fast, hard, unflinching...

Zarathustra notices the other's feet slowly sinking into the soft ground.

Conscientious of Spirit: ... gruesome, but conscientiously unbitten. O Zarathustra, that you once said "Spirit is the life that cuts itself to the quick" – that induced me and seduced me to your teachings. And truly, with my own blood I have grown by-my-self-knowledge!

Zarathustra notices the blood continuing to flow from the wounds on the other's forearm.

Zarathustra: Apparently so! You are uncanny, and how much I have learnt from this very demonstration! Seeing is believing, as they say, and you are the proof in the pudding itself. 'Tis plain to the eye. Leastways I should not have to rely on having everything drummed into your ears! Well then! Thus shall we part! But I should be glad to find you again. That way up there leads to my cave. There tonight you shall be my honoured guest. I should gladly make amends to your body, that Zarathustra once trod you underfoot! I shall ponder over the way. Now, however, a cry of distress calls me urgently hence.

Zarathustra bounds away.

6 – Exterior. Natural Amphitheatre. Morning

Zarathustra makes past a boulder, and sees the Enchanter, first writhing, then falling face down. Music portrays a motif very similar to the Great Cry of Distress, but very Wagnerian, and loud.

Zarathustra (*to himself, aside*): Gently! That there must be the Higher Man; from him that terrible cry of distress has been coming – I will see if anything can be done to help.

Zarathustra drops his stock and tries to put the Enchanter on his feet, but he seems to be insensible of anything around him.

Enchanter (*seemingly unable to stand, distant, forlorn; wracked by cramps of helplessness and distress*): Who warms me? Who is there to love me now? Give me warm hands! Warm the cockles of my heart.

Enchanter grabs and pins Zarathustra by the ankles. Zarathustra keeps his balance only by standing bolt upright, and leaving-off his attempts to help. He looks to the audience, deadpan.

Enchanter (*very melodramatic*): Quivering. Quaking. Cosy my feet like a dying flame – Racked, ah! From unknown fevers. Shivering from the tips of icy arrows. Stalked by thee, Unnameable! Hidden! Hideous!

Zarathustra, still pinned, looks to right and left, and over his shoulder, checking for danger.

Enchanter: Cloud-covered huntsman! Struck down by the lightning of thy mocking eye. (*lets go his hold on Zarathustra's ankles, and doubles-over into foetal position.*) Thus I lie, bent, rent, tormented by all the martyrs eternal – by thee, cruellest hunter, whoever thou art – ye god!

Zarathustra seems to be starting to feel pity for the Enchanter's torments.

Enchanter: Strike deeper! Strike one time more!

Zarathustra looks to his stock, as if with a good idea in mind.

Enchanter: Strike it through, break this heart! What good these martyrs with blunt-toothed arrows? Why watch again, O God, untiring of human anguish, with malicious joy lightning from thine eye? You choose not to kill, just to make martyrs – Martyrs? To make a martyr of me – Why? Whoever thou art, ye wanton god –

Zarathustra, seen from behind, squats to one knee, as if to tend the stricken man. Neither Zarathustra's hands, nor the Enchanter's head, can be seen.

Enchanter (*still seemingly insensible of Zarathustra's presence*): Aha! You creep closer? What do you want by such a midnight? Speak!

Zarathustra looks suspiciously up at the bright morning sun.

Enchanter: Ha! You're way too close – Go! Be gone!

Zarathustra squints suspiciously at the Enchanter.

Enchanter: Aha! Me – You want – me? Me – entire? – Aha! And if you make a martyr of me, foolthat you are, does that martyr-away my pride? Give me love – who's there to warm me? Who loves me now? – lend a hot hand ...

Zarathustra looks again to his stock.

Enchanter: ... Lend the cockles-of-a-heart. Give me – the Loneliest – the ice... Oh the burning ice! Give-over the foe himself, the learning of yearning for the foe! Give, yeah: *give way* – cruellest foe – give to me – thyself!

Zarathustra, increasingly unimpressed, picks up his stock and rises to his feet.

Enchanter (*still seemingly insensible of Zarathustra's presence*): Away! Thence he flew, my last single pleasure, my great foe... My John Doe, my gallows god! – (*with hands in the air, he walks on his knees, calling to the skies*) No! Come back, with all thy martyrs! To this last lonely soul. O come back! All the tracks of my tears run together for thee! (*cluching clasped hands to his chest*) And the last flame of my heart, it flickers for thee! O come back, whoever you are, My God! My Pain! My last – Happiness!
Zarathustra (*striking the Enchanter several blows with his cane, hard, as if to punctuate his words*): Hold it! Hold it! You showpony! You charlatan! You liar from the ground up! I know you well! I'll soon warm your heels for you, you sorcerer. I know just the thing to make things hot for the likes of you!
Enchanter: Hold off! Hold off! Strike no more, O Zarathustra! I'm playing it only for fun! Such things belong to my art. I wanted merely to try you on – as I tried-out this play. And verily, you've seen straight through me! But you too, O Zarathustra, you gave me a trying time of it just now. You are hard, you sage! You come down hard with your "truths". Indeed, your cane beat this very truth – out of me!
Zarathustra: Forget the flattery, you charlatan-from-the-ground-up! You're false: How can you talk about truth! You peacock of peacocks, you sea of vanity! What do you play me for, you sorcerer – What did you play for me there: In whom should I have believed when you yammered gramercy so?
Enchanter: *The Penitent of the Spirit,* that's who I played – you coined the phrase once yourself – the poet and enchanter, who ultimately turns his spirit against himself, and as one transformed, freezes to death from his own bad conscience and evil eye. And confess it, O Zarathustra, it took a long time for you to discover my artful deceptions! You believed in my distress as you cupped my head in your hands – I heard you yammer "too little love, he's been given too little love!" How my sweet malice rejoiced that I had seduced you to such extremes.
Zarathustra: You could have deceived more subtle minds than mine. I am not on guard against deceivers. Unguarded by necessity, that's my lot. But you! You deceive by necessity! I know you that much. You

have always to have double- triple- quadruple- quintuple-meaning! Even what you just confessed, to me, has long been neither true, nor false enough! You irredeemable counterfeiter, you can do no other. (*sarcastically clasps hands, as if to pray, and looks to heaven*) You would feign your very afflictions, though you were stood naked before thy physician. Thus you even dressed-up your lies here before me, claiming and declaiming "I'm playing it only for fun!" There was seriousness in it too: you *are* something of a Penitent-of-the-Spirit! I've worked you out, you're the enchanter of them all, but you've no deceit or conceit left for yourself. You're disenchanted with – and by – yourself! You've reaped-in nausea itself as your one genuine truth. Nothing about you rings true anymore, but ringing your mouth itself is nausea, and it sticks like mud.

Enchanter (*as if puffed up, in a jealous rage*): Who are *you* then! Who *dares* speak like that to me! *To me* – the greatest man alive! – (*as if deflated and suddenly drained*) O Zarathustra, I'm tired of it all. I'm sick of my arts. I'm not great. Why mis-take myself? But you know it well: I strove for the stars! I wanted to play *The Great Human Being*, and convinced many indeed – but the deception has gone beyond my powers. I'm being torn apart by it. O Zarathustra, everything about me is a lie, but that I am tearing apart – that part is real!

Zarathustra: It does you honour – it's to your honour that you sought greatness, but it betrays you too. You are not great, you awful old enchanter. That is your best and most honest trick – the one for which I can respect you: that you tired of yourself and proclaimed "I am not great". For that I honour you as a penitent-of-the-spirit. And if only for the wink-of-an-eye, in just this moment, you were for real. But tell me, what were you looking for in my fields and high mountains? And when you lay yourself across my path, what were you trying to do? Were you seeking – to lead me into temptation?

Enchanter: I didn't seek to tempt, I merely attempted to seek. You see, O Zarathustra, I seek the thing itself, the genuine article: upright, forthright, straight and simple in word and deed; a man of total honesty; a barrel of wisdom; a paragon of revelations – don't you know it, O Zarathustra, a great human being is what I seek, for namely, I seek you!

A long silence. Zarathustra, eyes closed, sinks deep within himself in thought.

Zarathustra (*with duplicitous eloquence*): Well then! That path up there leads the way to Zarathustra's cave. In there you might seek the one you would find. Ask my animals for advice, my eagle and my serpent: they will help you to look. My cave however, is great! I myself, frankly, have not seen any great human being. For what is great in man, even the eye of the most refined is nowadays too coarse. It is the rule of the mob. How many I have seen drawing on airs, puffing themselves up, and calling to the people "Behold! A great man!" But, as with all bags of wind, it's soon passed.

Satyrs, in the shadows, giggle like schoolboys.

Zarathustra: In the end, the bullfrog that puffs itself up too much – croaks (*blurts, then pulls a dead-face, then clasps hands piously*) and it's soon passed! To needle swollen windbags in the seat of their pride... (*Jabs the Enchanter in the bottom with the tip of his cane. The latter holds his backside and starts to run off*)... that's what I call a sharp way to shoot-the-breeze!

A fart is heard. Satyrs with sticks emerge to prod the Enchanter, one after the other, on his way around the stage. Each jab lands on the Enchanter's backside. Farting sounds and giggles punctuate the slapstick.

Zarathustra (*to the audience*): Did you hear that, you schoolboys? (*proclaiming, as if to the Enchanter*) This is the day of the rabble: Who knows, now, what is great – and what is small? Who today could strike it rich in search of greatness? Only some great golden fool, out after fool's gold!

The Satyrs leave off their mischief and look pointedly at Zarathustra.

Zarathustra: So you sought a great human being, you amazing fool? Who taught you that? Is this the time? O you hapless prospector... (*turns, and begins to bound away, smiling*)... why did you think me – a prospect?

7 – Exterior. Somewhere in the Mountains. Morning

Zarathustra, in high spirits, stops dead-in-his-tracks as he sees the Old Pope sitting up ahead, in his path.

Zarathustra (*to himself*): Woe is us, Old Heart, there sits unspeakable sorrow. It looks to me like something of a priestly sort. What does he want in my domain? Why, scarce am I escaped from the clutches of that Old Enchanter – must I now cross paths with another master of magic? another warlock and witch-doctor? another layer-on of hands and healer of the faith? a worker-of-miracles by the grace of God? an anointed defamer of the world – the Devil take him! But the Devil's never to be found when you need him. He's always one step behind – the painted rogue and lamefoot!

Zarathustra tries to leave the scene, but the Old Pope springs towards him, delighted.

Old Pope: Whoever you may be, good traveller, help one gone astray – a wanderer, an old man, who's in no little danger here, of harm! This world, to me, is alien and strange; I've heard the howling of wild beasts, and the one who might have offered me shelter here is, himself, no more. I sought the Last Pious Man, a holy man and hermit who, alone here in his backwoods, had not heard a whisper of what the whole world nowadays knows.
Zarathustra: What does the whole world nowadays know? Perhaps this: that the old God, in whom the whole world once believed, that he – lives no more?
Old Pope: You said it. And I served this old God right up to his final hour. Now, however, I've no-one to serve, no master, and yet I'm still not free, nor have a moment's happiness, except in reminiscence. That's why I climbed this mountain, so that I could finally celebrate a festival as becomes an old pontiff and father of the church: for, you should know, I am the last Pope! – Ah, a festival of pious memories and service to God. But now he himself is dead, this holyman of the forest, the Most Pious Man, who forever praised his god with atonal grumblings and song. The man himself, I could not find, when I found his hut – a couple of wolves were in it, however, behowling his death – for all beasts loved him, Amen. So I fled. Had I come in vain to these woods and high mountains? Well, there and then I set my heart on seeking out another, the most pious of all those who *don't* believe in God – on seeking Zarathustra!

Zarathustra (*grasping the other's hand*): Lo and behold, Your Venerability, what a lovely long hand! That is the hand of a dealer in blessings – eternal blessings. Now, however, it has a hold of the very occasion you sought, of me, Zarathustra. It is I, Zarathustra the Godless, he who once said "Who is it is more godless than I, that I may celebrate a share in his wisdom!"

Old Pope: Whoever beheld him and loved him most dearly, surely has now most sorely lost him – so behold! I myself am surely the most godless of the two? But what is there to celebrate in that?

Zarathustra: You served him to the end; you know how he died? Is it true, what they say, that he was strangled by his own pity; that he could see how mankind hung on the cross – and couldn't bear it – that his love for mankind became his Hell, and in the end, his death.

Long pause. The Old Pope bites his lip and turns aside.

Zarathustra: Let him go. Let him go; he is gone. And though it speaks well of you that you speak well of the dead, in this case you know as well as I who he was, and that he moved in mysterious ways. (*raises his eyebrows*)

Old Pope: Keep it under your hat, for in the affairs of God I am even more enlightened (*lifts his eyepatch and winks with his blind eye*) than Zarathustra himself – and have a right to be. My love (*rubs his backside, unconsciously*) served him many a long year, a willing slave to his will, to his every desire. A good servant knows everything (*with a knowing wink, aside:*) – and not a little besides – that his master hides from himself. He was a hidden god, full of secrecy. Why, he could get himself a son no other way than by the back door! Verily, at the very threshold to his faith – there adultery lies. Whoever praises him as a god of love thinks not high enough of Love itself. Did this god not want also to sit in judgement?

Zarathustra: Yet the lover loves beyond all requital and all reward...

Old Pope (*pensive*): When he was young, this oriental god of rising-suns was hard and vengeful and cast himself as the idol of his beloved people...

Zarathustra: ... by creating them a place called Hell!

Old Pope: Precisely! Ultimately, however, he grew old and soft and feeble and pitiful, more like a grandfather than a father, and most like a dithering old granny. There he sat, all dried-up, by the old pot-belly, stewing over his shaky knees, world-weary, wanting- and

good-for-nothing – and the day came where he simply up and suffocated – a victim of his own massive, overgrown pity.
Zarathustra: You old pontiff, have you seen all that with your own eyes? (*waves a hand on the Old Pope's blind side, as if to test his blindness*) It may well have gone that way indeed – that way or some other. For when gods die, you know, they die a thousand deaths. Well then! This way or that way, this way *and* that way – he is gone! Let him go! He rubbed my ears – and my eyes – up the wrong way, I shall say nothing more distasteful about him.

A fart is heard. Zarathustra rubs his nose.

Zarathustra: I love all that rings clear and speaks true. But he – you know it well, you old priest, there was something of *your* sort about him, something of a priestly manner – he was ambiguous. (*makes a very subtle gesture of effeminacy*) He was also obfuxious! (*listens for another noise*) How he would blow-up a storm with us, the old blowhard, that we found him hard to follow.

Another fart. Zarathustra looks over his shoulder, as if he fears himself to be the culprit.

Zarathustra: But why didn't he speak more clearly? And if the problem lay with our hearing, why did he give us such devilish ears? (*turns a finger in his ear, as if to clean it out*) If our heads were full of filth, well then! Who put it there? Why, if there was crock in the pot he'd be cranky, and crack-down on the pots, though it was him who'd cranked-out (*pauses to listen*) so many crocks. (*aside:*) The crackpot! – That's not just potty – it was a sin against good taste. And there is piety in good taste, you know. It was good taste that spoke-up and said "Enough! Away with such a god! Sooner no God, sooner to shape ones own fate on ones own wheel. (*turns a pirouette*) Sooner to be a fool. Sooner to be God oneself!" (*kicks up his heels*)
Old Pope: What did you say! O Zarathustra, you are more pious than you think with such impiety! Some sort of god in you has converted you to your Godlessness. Is it not your piety itself that denies you the belief in a God? And your monstrous honesty shall yet carry you off beyond good and evil!

A satyr and nymph enter in background. Lewd ballet ensues. Very sensuous.

Old Pope: And behold! What gobsmacking vistas lay open before you! You have eye and hand and mouth – (*aside:*) all open, I see – all pre-ordained as blessings, eternal blessings. (*grabs his crotch, unconsciously*) One does not bless with the hand alone. And, in your company – though you would like to be the most godless of all – I catch the scent of an uncanny fragrance – the incense of many long blessings...

Satyr is spraying petals, like confetti.

Old Pope: ... the sense of well-being. (*breathes deep*) Let me be your guest, O Zarathustra, just for a single night! Nowhere on Earth could I be more wholly-well, than with you.
Zarathustra: Amen! So it shall be! That path up there leads the way. Up there lies the cave of Zarathustra. I would gladly lead you the way myself, Your Venerableness, believe me, for I love all pious men. But now a cry of distress calls me urgently away. No one shall come to grief in my domain. My cave is safe haven, and indeed! above all I should like to set each and every bewailing shipwreck back on his feet and dry land. But who could take your burden (*crossing himself as he turns to leave*) from your shoulder? I am too weak for that. Long, truly, we shall have to wait – until someone resurrects your God for you, perhaps? That old God certainly lives no more. He is dead and buried – on good grounds! (*to the audience:*) Thus spake Zarathustra.

8 – Exterior. Sunlit Mountain Glade. Mid-Morning

Zarathustra alone.

Zarathustra (*light footed, cheerful*): What good things – what happy gifts this day has brought me! It's made amends for a bad beginning! What strange conversationalists I have met! And their words – I shall now mull them over awhile, as with kernels of sweet corn. Like grist to the mill I'll grind them husks-and-all, til like buttermilk they flow into my soul.

9 – Exterior. Gloomy Mountain Forest

The scene becomes eerie, gloomy, stark, sterile. Zarathustra slows his pace, then stops, as if unsure. The Ugliest Man gradually comes into sight. Zarathustra sees her and turns away with revulsion, then starts to run off.

Ugliest Man (*gives a thick, throaty cough*): Zarathustra! Zarathustra! Unriddle my riddle! Speak to me! Say, what is *The Revenge on the Witness?* I lure you back! Here is thin ice! Look out! See to it that your pride here doesn't break your back! – You think yourself wise, O haughty Zarathustra! Then unriddle the riddle, you hard cracker of hard nuts! The riddle that is me! Come, tell me who I am!

Zarathustra swoons, falls to one knee. Recovers.

Zarathustra: I know you well. You are the murderer – of God! Let me go. You couldn't bear it, that he saw you – that he saw through you, and always and everywhere – through and through – for you are *the Ugliest Man*. You took vengeance on him, as he was your witness!

Zarathustra turns to go, but the Ugliest Man latches on to his coat-tail.

Ugliest Man (*coughing horribly*): Stay! Stay! Don't pass me over! I divined the snare that brought you down to earth. Good health to you, O Zarathustra (*raises a glass*) that you're back on your feet! (*coughs*) You divined – how well I know – how it feels to be his killer – the murderer of God. Stay! Sit. Bide some time with me. It'll be no vain pursuit. To whom can I turn if not to you? Stay. Bide awhile. But don't look at me! Have some respect for my ugliness! – They hounded me. You now are my last resort. Not with their hate, not with their dogs – oh, such a pursuit I could treat with contempt and pride and a kicking-of-heels – has anything good ever come of a half-hearted pursuit? And he who pursues is soon merely a follower. (*looks over his shoulder*) Are they not well behind me! Yet they would always look out for me. They wanted to – pity! It's their pity from which I had no resort, but to you. To you, the only one who divined how it feels to be the one – who killed him. Stay! But if you are impatient, and must go, don't go the way I came. That way is no good. The path is a bad one.

Zarathustra is visibly uncomfortable.

Ugliest Man: Have I upset your applecart with all this metaphorically belaboured advice – speaking badly of the proverbial "way"? with my halting (*coughs up some phlegm*) humours? – But listen, I am it, the Ugliest Man – the one who plods, furthermore, with the greatest leaden feet. Wherever I tread the way, the path is always bad. I trudge every path to pieces and to death. That you, however, passed me by, in silence, that you blushed – I marked it well. By this I knew you to be Zarathustra. Anyone else would have tossed down their alms, their pity, their contemptuous charity in word and deed. But I am not beggar enough for that. You divined it. For that I am too rich. Too rich in that which is great. Too rich in that which is terrible, terrifying, hateful, ugly. In that which is ugliest, and unmentionable, most unmentionable. In that which is inexpressible, and beyond! Your sense of shame, O Zarathustra, it showed me respect! In a state of distress I escaped the throng of bleeding hearts, that I might find him, the only man today to teach that "Pity goes beyond the pale" – you, O Zarathustra! Be it divine, or be it the milk-of-human-kindness, pity has no sense of shame. And unwillingness to help can often be more noble than that virtue that imposes itself regardless. But charity! Charity nowadays ranks as virtue itself. The men-of-today – this dwarfish humanity – has no sense of awe at great misfortune, at great misadventure – at great ugliness. I look out, over and beyond all this, like a dog looking-out over-and-beyond the herd of bleating sheep. They are little, eager-to-help, eager-to-follow, weak-willed and willing people. For too long they have had their head – their rights, they call it, these little dwarves – so that ultimately they've taken over – they've taken the helm! Now they call the tune: "Good is what little people say is good" they say "and none besides." And Truth is what that preacher – that amazing holyman and advocate of humanity-writ-small preached, when – according to his own testimony – he stood-up and said "I – am the Truth!" Such immodest presumption has long since puffed-up the coxcomb of the cock-sparrow mob. "I am the Truth and the Way," he taught them. And yeah-verily-yeah it was no trifling blunder to teach! But has a pretender-to-the-throne ever been more richly rewarded? You, however, O Zarathustra, you passed him over and said "No! No! and No again!" You pointed-out the error of his ways. You as the first of them gave warnings of Pity – not to one-and-all, but to you-and-yours. You were ashamed of the shame of great suffering, and truly, when you said "A great cloud of Pity is approaching, look-out you men one-and-all!" – when you taught that "All creators are hard" and that "All great love is beyond Pity" – O Zarathustra, how well-versed you seemed to me at forecasting the weather! – But you yourself – you must now warn yourself of your Pity! For there are many on their way to you. Many suffering, doubting, hopeless, drowning, freezing – I must even warn you of myself. You divined my best, my most devious riddle – Who I am – and What I did. I know the bait that brings you down. Yet he had to die. He saw with eyes that saw all. He saw humanity to the depths and from the ground up, all its shame and ugliness. His pity new no shame. He crawled into my dirtiest crannies. One such as him – overcurious, over-imposing, over-pitying – he had to die. He always saw me. On such a witness I had to have revenge – or not live myself. The god that saw everything – even ones humanity – this god had to die! Humanity could not suffer it, if such a witness lived on.

Zarathustra (*as if chilled to the bone*): You are inexpressible, ineffable, and you did warn me of your ways. As thanks, allow me to recommend mine to you. Behold, that way up there lies the cave of Zarathustra. My cave is great and deep and has many nooks. There are niches for even the most fugitive recondite. And hard by it are hundreds of intriguing loop-holes and wormholes for the more flighty, or jumpy, or slow-crawling creatures. You outcast, you've cast yourself out and beyond the life of men and human pity! Well then, you do as I do! You learn from me. Only in doing does one learn in-deed. And speak first-and-foremost with my animals! The proudest beast and the cleverest beast – they may well be the best advisors for us both!

10 – Exterior. Gloomy Mountain Forest

Zarathustra alone.

Zarathustra (*walking, reflective*): How poor mankind is even now! How ugly and croaky. How full of hidden shame! They tell me humanity is love of humanity. Oh how much it must love itself then! How much scorn it has up against it! With him, too, his self-contempt betrayed his self-love – he is, to me, a great drainer of love's cup – a great pourer of scorn.

The sound of a mighty waterfall is building.

11 – Exterior. Precipice and Waterfall. Mid-Morning

Zarathustra alone, walks across a very narrow bridge, apparently oblivious of the sheer drop and raging torrent below him.

Zarathustra: (*reflective*) I've never found anyone with a deeper scorn – and the depth marks the height! (*stops mid-span*) Woe, perhaps he was the Higher Man? Was he the one I heard? I love a great scorner. (*walks on*) Humanity however, is something that must be overcome. (*steps off the bridge, and hugs himself, as if against a deep chill*)

12 – Exterior. Montage. Various Terrain. Late-Morning

Zarathustra wanders over hill-and-dale, meadow and stony ground.

13 – Exterior. Mountain Pasture. Late-Morning

Zarathustra steps from a rocky outcrop onto grassy pasture.

Zarathustra (*as if suddenly warmed, and unburdened*): But what has happened to me? Something living and warm quickens my soul, it must be nearby. Suddenly I am not so alone. Unsuspected companions are losing themselves with me. The warmth of their breath wafts all around and settles into my soul.

The Voluntary Beggar

Zarathustra looks all around and sees a few cows huddled together in the meadow. He springs zealously into the huddle, as if to save the person in its midst. The huddle of cows parts to reveal the Voluntary Beggar, sitting.

Zarathustra: What are you doing here?
Voluntary Beggar: What am I doing here? Why, the same as you, you peacebreaker, I'm looking for happiness on Earth. I might have learnt something about it too, from these cows – for you should know, I've been talking to them half the morning, and they were just about to give me a little something. Why did you disturb them? For if we do not mend our ways and become as cows, we shall never come into the Kingdom of Heaven. We must learn this one thing from them – to be specific – namely, chewing-the-cud. And verily, even if humanity conquered the entire world, but failed to learn this one thing – chewing-the-cud – what good would it do! We should still not be free of our misery, our great misery – Nausea, they call it nowadays. Who today has not had a heart-, mouth-, and eyeful of nausea? You too! Even you! But look again at these cows! (*takes his eyes off the cows for the first time, looks at Zarathustra, and jumps up with a start*) Who's this I'm speaking with? Why, this is the man without nausea! Zarathustra himself! The conqueror of The Great Nausea. This is the eye, (*punctuates each word with a kiss of Zarathustra's hand*) this the mouth, this the heart of Zarathustra!

The cows are astonished.

Zarathustra (*pulling away*): Speak not of me, you amazing, you lovely fellow – tell me about you! Are you not the Voluntary Beggar, who once threw away a great fortune? who was ashamed of his riches – and the rich – and fled to the poorest-of-the-poor, to give them his hand and heart – but they didn't take him in.
Voluntary Beggar: But they didn't take me in – you'd better know it; so ultimately I turned to the animal kingdom, and these cows.
Zarathustra: There you learned how it is harder to give things the right way than to take things the right way, and that good-giving is an art, and a trap for young players.
Voluntary Beggar: Especially today, where everything humble is coy, and rides a high horse – in revolt against one thing or another – quite particular, in fact, and not just generally revolting, the way they used to be. For the hour is come – you know it well – for the great big-

bad long-and-slow slave revolt and rising-tide of the rabble – it grows and grows! Passionate greed, bitter envy, resentful scorn, rag-tag pride: all was thrown in my face. It's no longer true that the poor are at all bless̄ed. The Kingdom of Heaven, however, is with the cows.

The cows, with upturned noses, sniff and snort at the Voluntary Beggar.

Zarathustra (*holding the cows back from the Voluntary Beggar*): And why is it not with the rich?
Voluntary Beggar (*gradually working himself-up into a sweat*): Why prod and probe? You know better than I do what drove me to the dirtiest of the poor. Was it not nausea at the filthiest of the rich? They're all shysters, you know – cold eyed and lustful, turning misery – to profit. Riff-raff! Heaven itself reeks from their public airings – they're a gilded rabble! Hypocrites! Their fathers were pickpockets and parasites. They were rag-pickers then, and they're rag-pickers now. Rabble above, rabble below! Rich, poor – it's less than a label, you know. I have unlearned the difference. I've distanced myself from the entire muchness – further and further – until I reached these cows. (*at a peak of agitation, begins to snort – sounding just like the cows*)

The cows are amazed.

Zarathustra (*shaking his head and smiling to himself*): You do yourself violence with such harsh words – with such a sermon – on this mount. Your mouth wasn't made for such severity, nor your eyes – nor, as I think, your stomach neither. They contradict every word of such anger. You're not-a-one for such hatred and rabid distemper. Your stomach needs softer things – you were just not built for shredding flesh. Far sooner I think you a fruit-and-root man. Do you munch corn? Anyway, I am sure you shun the pleasures of flesh – and have a soft spot for honey!
Voluntary Beggar (*very seriously*): You read me well. I love honey, and munch corn too. And I seek that which cleanses the palate and leaves the breath fresh – also, that which takes forever – something to get ones teeth into while shooting-the-breeze, let's say. These cows, to be sure, have taken it the furthest: they've discovered chewing-the-cud, and lying in the sun. (*as if imparting a great secret*) Furthermore, they eschew all heavy considerations – nothing that might put-the-wind-up, or cause the heart to burn.

The Shadow

Zarathustra: Well then! You shall see my animals too – my eagle and my serpent – they have nothing-on-Earth to equal them. Behold! That way up there is the path to my cave. Be my guest there tonight, and talk with my animals about the contentment of cows – 'til I come home! For now, a cry-of-distress calls me urgently away. Fresh honey, too, you'll find there, and ice-cold golden honeycomb – eat your fill! Now, however, take it on the hoof!

The cows are pressing heavily on the Voluntary Beggar.

Zarathustra: It's time to leave your cows, you amazing, you golden-hearted fellow – though it may make you a little dour to leave your warmest friends and teachers of wisdom!
Voluntary Beggar: With one exception – and one I'd rather take to – O Zarathustra, is you yourself. You yourself are good, and even better than a cow!
Zarathustra: Away! Away with you, you sweet-talking drone. Do you want to spoil me with such honey-sweet spittle? Buzz off! Get away!

Zarathustra swings his stock at the Voluntary Beggar, who runs off at top speed.

14 – Exterior. Mountain Pasture. Late-Morning

Shadow (*calling from some distance behind Zarathustra*): Wait! Zarathustra! Wait a minute! It's me, O Zarathustra! Me, your shadow!
Zarathustra: What's happened to my solitude? It's getting way too crowded for me up here. These mountains are swarming. My kingdom is no longer of this world. I need a new horizon! Is that my shadow calling me? So what? What lies in my shadow? If it must follow me, I – shall run away!

Zarathustra runs off, the Shadow in hot pursuit.

15 – Exterior. Mountain Ridge. Late-Morning

The Voluntary Beggar, Zarathustra, and the Shadow are seen from a distance, in silhouette, running one-behind-the-other along the ridge.

Zarathustra (*voice over*): How now! Have not the most laughable things always happened amongst us old hermits and holymen? Verily, my folly has grown high in the mountains! Why, now I'm hearing footsteps – the pitter-patter of six tiny old-fool's-feet! But is it right for Zarathustra to be afraid of a shadow? Besides, in the final analysis, I think you'll find he has longer legs than I do.

16 – Exterior. Mountain Ridge. Late-Morning

Zarathustra stops dead-in-his-tracks, and turns around. Shadow collides head-on with Zarathustra, and falls like a shadow to the ground.

Zarathustra: Who are you? What are you doing here? And why do you call yourself my shadow? I don't like the look of you at all.
Shadow (*without melodrama*): Forgive me that I am. And if you find me unsightly, well then! O Zarathustra! In that I can praise you and your good taste. I am a wanderer. All-too-often I've got under your feet. Always on the go, but with no goal at all – nor any home – so that truly I am not far short of the Eternal Jew, except that I am not eternal – nor even a Jew.

Satyrs & maenads, in the background, have begun a ballet, playing out a dumb-show of the Shadow's speech.

Shadow (*as before*): How now! Must I always be on the go, then? Whirled by every wind, restless, driven on. O World, how you've turned me 'round-and-round! On every surface I have sat. Like weary dust I've slept on mirrors and windowpanes. Everything takes from me, nothing gives. I've become thin – why, I'm starting to look like a shadow! You, however, I followed longest and strongest, O Zarathustra. And if I hid myself from you, then still I was your best shadow. Where you but cast a glance, there I cast my lot. With you I have been abroad in the coldest, most far-fetched worlds – like a ghost that flits will-o-the-wisp over snow-tops and roof-scapes. With you I have striven in everything most difficult and distant, and if anything about me could be called Virtue, it would be this: that I feared no prohibition! With you I shattered all that my heart held dear. I overthrew every boundary-stone and idol. I pursued the most dangerous desires. Truly, over every transgression I have bounded at least once. With you I unlearned the belief in words and values and great names. When the Devil sheds his skin does his name not come away too? Perhaps skin is – the Devil himself! "Nothing is True – Everything is allowed" – that's what I said to myself. In to the coldest water I plunged myself, heart-and – head! Oh, how often I found myself standing there naked, as red as a lobster! Oh whence did I come by everything good and worth blushing about? Whence my belief in the righteous! Oh whence is that dissembled innocence that I once had – the innocence of the Righteous and their noble lies? Too often, truly, I followed hard-on-the-heels of Truth: it stood me on my head. Often I meant only to lie, and behold! There first I struck on – the truth! Too much exposed itself to me – now not a bar of it goes to my heart. Nothing now lives, that I love – how should I still love – myself?

Zarathustra seems non-plussed. The Shadow has found a human skull, but is totally unaware of the Shakespearean quality of his speech.

Shadow (*as before*): To be – to live life as I have a lust for it – or not to be – not to live at all – that's how I will have it. That's how the holiest of the holies would have it too. But woe! How can I still have – lust? Do I still have a goal? A haven for which my sails are set? A fair wind? Alas – only those who know where they're headed, know too, which winds their headwinds are, and which winds are fair.

Zarathustra becomes increasingly sombre.

Shadow: What's left for me now? A heart racy and tired. A restless will. Flighty wings. A broken back. This homesickness, O Zarathustra, this search for a home of my own – you know it well – this search has been a sickness – it has consumed me. "Where is my home?" I ask and seek and have sought. I have not found it. Eternally everywhere. Eternally nowhere. Eternally – in vain!

Zarathustra (*with genuine sympathy*): Thou art my shadow. (*lays a hand on the other's shoulder*) Your danger is no small one, you free spirit and wanderer! You have had a bad day – see to it that an even worse night doesn't befall you! Wretches like you find, ultimately, even prisons a blessing. Have you ever seen a fugitive sleep-off his capture? He sleeps tight. There's a sort of peacefulness and pleasure in his newfound sanctuary. Guard yourself against it, lest in-the-end you too become imprisoned by some narrow faith – some hard-and-fast delusion! It's precisely you who stands most to be seduced and induced to anything straight and narrow. You have lost your goal – woe, how should you have made good – or even light – of your loss? How to go on? To laugh? To cry? Thus you lost, also, your way! You poor gull, you butterfly, you – gadfly! Would you like a hearth and home for the evening? Then go on up to my cave! That path there leads the way! But for now I feel the need, quickly, to run away from you again. I feel – it's like there's a shadow cast over me. I wish to go it alone, now, so that everything about me again becomes clear and light. For that, I have yet awhile to be light on my feet. This evening, however, we shall dance.

17 – Exterior. Montage. Various Terrain. Forenoon

Zarathustra, alone, runs and runs for hours, encountering no one. He becomes increasingly exhilarated and refreshed.

18 – Exterior. Elysian Field. Midday

Zarathustra comes upon a beautiful meadow, and notices an old tree, wound about by a vine laden with ripe and ripening grapes. He stops to quench his thirst, but in reaching for a grape, is overcome by an even stronger urge – to rest. He lies down by the tree and sleeps, eyes wide open and fixed on the vine above.

Zarathustra (*voice over*): Hush! Hush! Is the world not just now – perfect? What has happened to me? Like a gentle breeze, unseen, dancing on sheltered seas, light as a feather – sleep dances upon me.

Noon

She turns me no blind eye. She leaves my soul awake. Truly, she is light – light as a feather. She coaxes me over – I know not how. She daubs me inwardly with flattering hand. She brings me – Yea, she takes me over – my soul spreads herself wide.

Satyrs and nymphs have emerged to dance, in pairs, the coniunctio. Zarathustra is still motionless. Zarathustra's Soul dances alone.

Zarathustra (*voice over: as if working-up to a serenade*): How long and weary she has become, my beguiling soul! Has the evening of some seventh day come to her here at the very stroke of noon?

The dance of the satyrs and nymphs alternates between the coniunctio and the danse macabre.

Zarathustra (*voice over: as if serenading his soul*): Has she wandered too long among good and ripe things? She spreads herself wide. She stretches far, long – longer! Still she lies, my beguiling soul. She has tasted too much of the good; this golden melancholy presses her; her lips – they quiver. Like the ship running home to cove – by still waters – now resting itself against the earth, weary of the long journey and the uncertain sea – yea, the earth is more faithful – where the ship hugs the land, lovingly, there tis enough that a spider spin its web betwixt them – no stronger cord need be struck. Thus, like the weary ship in the stillest alcove, I too now rest here close by the earth, faithful, full of faith, waiting; bound to her by the lightest of cords. – O Happiness! O My Soul! Don't you want to sing? You lie in the grass. Yet it is the uncanny, solemn, auspicious hour, where no herd plays his flute. Shame on thee! Burning Midday sleeps on the green. No songs now! Hush! The world is perfect.

The dance has carried all the dancers but Zarathustra's Soul from the stage. She is alone with the sleeping Zarathustra, and is peeking at him longingly from behind the tree-trunk.

Zarathustra (*voice over*): No songs, you grasshopper, my soul! Not a whit! Not a flap! But behold – be still! the old midday sleeps, he cups his mouth – has he not just drunk a drop of happiness – an olden golden drop of sparkling luck, of golden wine? It flits upon him, his happiness laughs. Thus – laughs a god. Hush!

Zarathustra's Soul begins to dance a graceful solo.

Zarathustra (*voice over*): "For Happiness – how little one needs for Happiness!" Thus I spoke once, and thought myself clever. But it was a blunder-bug; the Moment has taught me that – this moment. Clever fools speak better. The littlest thing, the quietest, lightest – the rustling of a lizard, a sigh, a whisper, the-wink-of-an-eye – little is the very stuff of the best happiness. Hush!

Zarathustra's Soul returns again and again to Zarathustra's sleeping form, as if yearning for him to get up and dance with her.

Zarathustra (*voice over*): What happened to me – listen! Has Time itself flown away? Am I not falling? Have I not fallen – listen! into the fountain of Eternity? – What is happening to me? Hush! It cuts me – woe! – to the heart? To the heart! O break, break Heart, for such happiness; from such a cut! – How now! Has the world not just become perfect? Round and ripe? O the golden rounded ring – to where has it flown? I shall chase it down! Still! – Hush.

Zarathustra's Soul runs from the stage, as if searching for something. Zarathustra's eyes close for the first time, and he nods with sleep. This seems to rouse him a little, and he sits up, eyes still closed.

Zarathustra (*voice over*): Up! You slacker! You day-dreamer! Well then, let's go, my old legs! The time has come, it's High Time, and many good parts of the way are still left for your return. Now you sleep yourself out, but for how long? Half an eternity! Well then, let's go, my old Heart! How long shall you need, to bring yourself 'round, after a sleep like that?

Zarathustra lays back down, eyes still closed, asleep. Zarathustra's Soul is discovered, awake, smiling, lying happily at his side, holding a bouquet of golden flowers to her heart with both hands.

Zarathustra Soul (*voice over: singing sweetly, gently, as in a lullaby*): Leave me then! Hush! Has the world not just now become perfect? O the golden rounded ball!

Zarathustra (*voice over*): Get up, you little vixen! you time-killer! How now? Still stretching, yawning, sighing, falling-back under deep fountains? Yet who are you! O my Soul!

A ray of sunlight falls across Zarathustra's face, and he wakes with a start. Zarathustra's Soul is gone, and he is seen from a height, looking up, still lying.

Noon

Zarathustra (*voice over*): O Heavens above, do you see me? Do you hear my beguiling soul? When will you drink this drop of dew fallen upon all earthly things – when will you drink this beguiling soul – when, Fountain of Eternity! you terrible Abyss of the Noontide – when will you drink my soul back into – thyself?

Zarathustra springs to his feet, as if returning to himself from some uncanny dream.

Act Two

19 – Exterior. Zarathustra's Cave. Late afternoon

Zarathustra, returning home, nears the boulder at the mouth of his cave, when suddenly a great ruckus is heard from within. "The Great Cry of Distress" motif resounds in the orchestra. Zarathustra leaps to the entrance.

20 – Interior. Zarathustra's Cave. Late afternoon

Zarathustra's Eagle and Serpent stand back-to-back amid a throng of questioning guests. The eagle's feathers are visibly ruffled. The guests – the Old Prophet, the Kings to Right and Left, the Conscientious of Spirit, the Enchanter, the Old Pope, the Ugliest Man, the Voluntary Beggar, and the Shadow – are actually seated, but seem to be pressing in upon the eagle and serpent with the importunity of their interrogations. The Ugliest Man is wearing a crown and two purple robes. Right and Left are bare-headed and in long-johns. The mule is seated with the others.

21 – Interior. Zarathustra's Cave. Late Afternoon

As Zarathustra appears from the entrance, the guests a fall silent and stand. The eagle and serpent take the opportunity to flee. Zarathustra steps to the middle and looks penetratingly into the eyes of each guest in turn, as if reading faces.

Zarathustra: You doubters! You amazing men! So it was *your* cry of distress I heard? And now I know, too, where he is to be found – the one I sought today in vain – the Higher Man. In my own cave he sits, the Higher Man! But litt e wonder – did I not lure him here myself, spruiking happiness with samples of honey, and cunning catch-calls? –

The Homecoming

But now, I think, you're not the best of company! Why, left to your own devices, you're making each other's hearts sink with these cries of distress. Someone is missing – someone who can make you laugh again, a jolly good buffoon, a wild beast and wind and dancer, some or other old fool – what do you think? – Forgive me, though, you doubters, that I speak so bluntly to your faces – unworthy, truly, of such guests! But you have not-a-whit divined what it is encourages my heart. Why you yourselves do it – and your long faces! Forgive it of me, but who is it can help but take heart, who looks upon a doubter? To speak well to doubters – everybody is certain enough of themselves for that! You yourselves have given me the power – a good gift, my lofty friends! A good, upstanding, house-warming gift! Well then, don't begrudge it me that I offer you something of mine in return. This here is my domain. Here I am master. That which is mine, however, for this evening and this night, shall be yours too. My animals shall serve you. My cave shall be your refuge. None shall be doubters here with me in my own house. Why, in this ward, even your own wild beasts shall not reach you. And that is the first thing I offer you here – Safety! The second however is – my little finger! And once you have taken that, well then! Help yourselves to my entire hand – and my whole heart too! (*Zarathustra goes among the others locking fingers, shaking hands, patting backs, laughing etc.*)
Welcome! Welcome to my home! Be my guests!

The guests all bow down and shrink back again, as if in awe.

Right: O Zarathustra, the way you gave us your hand and Hellos – *thus* we recognized you as Zarathustra. You lowered yourself before us; you almost did violence to our awe – who else would be able, however, to lower himself with such pride as you? That itself set us on our feet, a balm to our eyes and hearts. To see this alone, we would have climbed higher mountains than this mountain is. We came precisely as sightseers, we wanted to see what could make sad eyes clear – and behold! it's already a thing of the past – all our cries of distress. Our hearts and minds are opened already, and made bright. There's really little left to be desired – even our courage is encouraged. Nothing on Earth, O Zarathustra, grows more joyfully than a lofty, strong will – that is her most beautiful outgrowth. An entire landscape rejoices at such a tree. Like an oak, O Zarathustra, one who like you grows tall, silent, hard, alone; of the best, most

flexible timber; splendid – ultimately, however, reaching out with strong green branches for his domain, asking hard questions of wind and weather and whatever is a ways strange about the heights – even harder in answer, a master, victorious – oh, who wouldn't climb into high mountains to see such outgrowths of earth? And truly, many eyes are turned, today, to your mountain and treetop. A great longing has raised itself up, and many have learned to ask: Who is Zarathustra? And when once you trickled your song and your honey into their ears, all the hidden hermits and loners spoke at once to their hearts: "Is Zarathustra still alive? There's no reason to live anymore; life has no meaning; it's all in vain unless – unless we might live with Zarathustra!" – "Why doesn't he come?" they ask, "he who has so long seemed on his way?" – "Has the solitude engulfed him? Or is there a way to him yet?" Now it occurs to us that solitude itself has become brittle and broken, like a grave broken open and pouring forth its dead. The resurrected are swarming. And now the waves about your mountain are climbing and climbing, O Zarathustra. And however high your height may be, there's no shortage of those who need to take a rise – out of you! Your ark shall soon be – err – not so high and dry. For he himself is underway and on his way to you – the last remnant of God among men: the man of the Great Longing, that is; the man of the Great Nausea, of the Great Saturation – the man who doesn't want to live, but that he learns to hope again – but that he learns from you, O Zarathustra, the great hopefulness!
(*takes Zarathustra's hand and tries to kiss it*)
Zarathustra (*astonished, pulls away and seems distant for a moment, then returns his gaze to his guests*): My guests, you Higher Men, I will speak straight and in plain English. I have not been waiting here in these mountains for you...
Left (*aside*): Straight and in plain English? God save us from that! I see this sage from the east knows nothing of the English! What he really means is "plain and simple" – Well then! That, nowadays, is not in the worst of taste!
Zarathustra: You, all-of-you, may well be higher men, but for me you are not nearly high, nor mighty enough. For me, that is. For that which is merciless. For that which I shall not say – for it is merciless – though I shall not remain silent forever. And if you do belong to me, you do not belong to me so much as my right arm! Whoever stands on sick and shaky egs, like you, wants first and foremost – whether

he knows it or not, or perhaps hides it from himself – he wants to be spared. My arms and legs, however, I do not spare. I shall not spare my warriors. How then, could you fight my battles? Every victory with you would be, to me, a wet one. And not-a-few of you would go to pieces at the mere sound of my drums! Besides, you are not beautiful enough, nor well-born. I need pure, perfect mirrors for my images; on your surface, my teachings would become grotesque. Your shoulders carry many burdens, many memories; many misshapen dwarves limp in your darkest caves. There is a hidden rabble in you too. And though you be high, and perhaps of a higher sort, much about you is nevertheless crooked and ugly. There's no smith in the world could hammer you straight and true enough for me. To me, you are bridges. May there be higher than you come to clamber across! You have meaning as steps, so don't be upset at those who clamber all over you on the way to the top! From your seed a true son and consummate heir may well grow for me too – but that is far off. You yourselves are not those to whom my name and inheritance belongs. I have not been waiting in these mountains for you. It's not with you that I can, for the last time, descend. You are merely good omens that yet higher men are on their way – not those of the Great Longing, of the Great Nausea, of the Great Saturation, and that which you call *the Remnants of God*. No! No! Thrice No! I wait in these mountains for others – and will not budge a foot from here without them – for higher, stronger, more uplifted, more optimistic; such as are built upright in body and soul – laughing lions must come! O my dear guests, you amazing men – have you not heard of my children? And that they are on their way to me? Why don't you speak to me of my garden, of my blessed islands, of my beautiful new species. As your housewarming gift I should like to beg this of your warmth: that you speak to me of my children. In *that* I am rich. In *that* I have become poor. What wouldn't I give for this one thing: to have my children with me? These living specimens, these living outgrowths and oak-trees of my will and my highest hopes!

22 – Interior. Zarathustra's Cave. Early-Evening

Enchanter (*very animated, rushes to the fore and takes Zarathustra's hand*): But Zarathustra! One thing is more necessary than another! You say so yourself. Well then, one thing is now more necessary to me than anything else – timing is everything, you know – and didn't you invite me here to a meal? In fact, there are many of us here who have come a long way. Surely you don't mean to feed-us-up on proverbs and lip-service alone? Everyone seems to have given too much thought to drowning, freezing, choking-to-death, and other bodily distress, but no-one seems to have had a care for my particular bodily distress, namely, starvation...

Zarathustra's pets flee in horror as the Enchanter hungrily eyes them off.

Enchanter: ... dying of thirst into-the-bargain. And though I hear water babbling in here, the dictates of wisdom seem to be babbling too – namely overflowing and requiring a cork! But I'd like a little wine! Not everyone is, like Zarathustra, a born water-drinker. Water's no good for those who're weary and worn. Wine's what's wanted for the likes of us! Wine alone induces sudden recuperation and impromptu health!

Left: For wine – well, we've taken care of that – me and my brother, the King to the Right. We have wine enough – an entire mule-skin full. So there's nothing to be desired, but bread.

Zarathustra: Bread? Hermits don't exactly have bread, but man doesn't live by bread alone – rather by the flesh of good little lambs, of which I have two – take them now! slaughter them and spice them up – that's how I like it!

Zarathustra's pets begin to bring-in food. Throughout the following, the guests all help themselves.

Zarathustra: And we're not short of rootstock and fruitstock, for those with a taste for fine flavours, nor of nuts and other riddles to crack. It won't take long for us to make a good meal of it. But whoever wants to eat must lend a hand too – even the kings! With Zarathustra, even a king can be cook.

Voluntary Beggar (*jovially*): Listen to this connoisseur Zarathustra! Does a man go into caves and high mountains to make a meal such as

this? Now I begin to understand what he once taught us – "Praised be a little poverty!" – and why he would abolish beggars.
Zarathustra: Be good now, you splendid fellow, like me – and grind your corn, drink your water, praise your own palate, as long as it makes you happy! I am a law only unto myself – I lay no law unto the land. (*begins to deftly illustrate each point by snatching or juggling items of food, or cooking utensils*) But whoever belongs to me and mine, they need marrow and spine – meat on the bone – and light on their feet; with an appetite for great wars and great festivals; no stick-in-the-mud, no head-in-the-cloud; as ready for hardships as feast-days, healthy and whole. The best belongs to mine and me – and if they withhold it from us (*snatching a berry from one of the kings*), then we take it – the best of food, the purest skies, the strongest thoughts, the most beautiful women! (*makes eyes at the Ugliest Man*)
Right: Strange! Did anyone ever hear such clever things from the lips of a sage? And truly, that is the strangest thing there could be about a sage: that he could be clever about everything, and not a complete ass.
Mule: Ye-ah!

23 – Interior. Zarathustra's Cave. Evening

Zarathustra moves about sampling the food, and helping the others in its preparation. They all eat heartily and seem to be enjoying themselves as he holds forth.

Zarathustra: When I went among men for the first time, I committed the folly of all hermits, the Great Folly – I stood myself in the marketplace! And in speaking to all, I spoke to none. In the evening, however, acrobats were my companions – and corpses – and I myself well nigh a corpse. With the new morning, however, a new truth dawned upon me. I learned there and then to say "What business of mine is the marketplace and the rabble and the raucous crowd, with their long ragamuffin ears! (*looks unintentionally at the mule*) You Higher Men, learn this from me: in the marketplace no-one believes in higher men. And if you speak there, well then! The mob, however, blinks – "We are all equal, you Higher Men" – thus blink the rabble – "there are no higher men, we are all the same. Man is man, in the eyes of God – we are all equal!" – In the eyes of God! – but now this God is dead. In the eyes of the rabble, however, we do not wish to be all the same. You Higher Men, steer clear of the marketplace!

24 – Interior. Zarathustra's Cave. Evening

The scene resembles an intemperate cooking class.

Zarathustra: In the eyes of God! Now, however, this God is dead! You Higher Men, this God was your greatest danger. Only since he has lain in his grave, are you – for the first time – resurrected. Now, for the first time, comes the Great Noontide. Now, for the first time, the Higher Man comes to be Lord and Master! O my brothers, do you understand this word? You are horrified? Your hearts shudder, feint and false? The abyss gapes before you? The Hell-hound howls – the Hell-hound in you! – Well then! Let's go, you Higher Men! Now for the first time we go from the sublime to the – future-of-mankind! God died: now it is our will that the Superman live.

25 – Interior. Zarathustra's Cave. Evening

Zarathustra approaches a new dish.

Zarathustra: The biggest question today: "How is Humanity to be preserved?" – Zarathustra asks, however, as the first and only: "How is humanity to be overcome?" – The Superman is what I have at heart, he is my first and only – and not humanity, not my neighbour, not the poor, not those who suffer – nor my nearest and dearest – nor the best. O my brothers, that which I can love in man is that he is a way up and over, a way to the eventide too; a dawning and a going-down. And there is much in you that drives me to – hope and love. There is much to honour in you, that you have doubts, that you have not learned how to give yourselves up, to sell yourselves out, to become devotees and dedicated – you have not learned the craft of the Little Cleverness. For today – precisely (*adds a pinch of salt – with exaggerated precision – to the dish before him*) – little people have become master. They preach dedication and modesty and cleverness and hard-work and helpfulness, and the long drawn-out and-so-on of the little virtues. They ask and ask, and never tire of the question: "How can humanity preserve itself – for the best, for the longest, most pleasantly?" Thus they are the men of the moment, the masters of the day. – Overcome them – these lords temporal, O my brothers – these little people – they are the Superman's greatest danger. Overcome the little virtues, I say – the crafty little cleverness, the business nose – the busy-ness body – the glad-hand for everyone (*smilingly feeds the mule a carrot, then hits it with his stick*); smug contentment, pitiable self-satisfaction, "the happiness of the greatest number!" And better to doubt, than to give yourselves up to some little dedication. And truly, you Higher Men, I love you for it, that you don't know how to live in this day-and-age. (*feigns bewilderment at the variety of dishes looming before him*) Thus, precisely, do you live – for the best! (*quickly picks a morsel from each dish and, tossing them high, juggles them into his mouth*)

26 – Interior. Zarathustra's Cave. Evening

Zarathustra approaches a new dish.

Zarathustra: Do you have courage, O my brothers? Are you brave? Not courage before witnesses, but the courage of hermits and eagles? the courage that goes unseen by God and man? The cold heart, the donkey, the blind-man, the drunkard – there's no courage in that. He is brave who knows fear, but overcomes it; who sees the abyss, but with pride – who sees the abyss, but with eagle's eyes and who, with eagle's claws – gets a grip (*takes a fist-full of his own hair in each hand*) on the abyss: *He* – has courage.

27 – Interior. Zarathustra's Cave. Evening

Zarathustra approaches a new dish.

Zarathustra: "Mankind is evil" – thus spoke all the wisest of men in trying to console me. Ah, but if only it were still true today! Evil, you see, is mankind's most powerful engine. "Mankind must become more evil. Better is *badder*." That's what I teach! The greatest evil *is necessary* to the Superman's greatest good. – It may well have been good for that preacher of the little people that he suffered and strove under the burden of human sin – I, on the other hand, rejoice in the greatest of sins as my greatest of consolations. Such things, however, are not said for those with long ears (*looks to the mule, who is grazing on some beautifully prepared dishes*). And some words are simply stupid in the wrong mouth.

The mule looks up, his mouth covered with a lather of cream.

Zarathustra: But these are delicate, distant things. The hooves of sheep will never be able to grasp them.
Mule: Ye-ah!

28 – Interior. Zarathustra's Cave. Evening

Zarathustra goes over and samples the creamy dish just munched by the mule – and winces at the taste.

Zarathustra (*laughing at his own folly*)**:** You need a healthy mistrust about you nowadays, you Higher Men. You show a great deal of heart, but perhaps you're too open-hearted? Keep your reasons to yourself! Today – it belongs to the rabble. What the rabble once came to believe without rhyme or reason: who could turn them out of that – with reasoning? In the marketplace, gestures are convincing (*deftly juggles a few pieces of fruit, then holds them up, as if for sale*). But reasons – reasons make rabble mistrustful. And even if, one day, a truth did come to be victorious: you would be a thousand times right to ask – with your healthy mistrust – "What powerful error has done battle here, to gain just this victory?" – Beware of learnéd men! They hate you, for they bear no fruit.

All look pointedly at the Conscientious of Spirit, who has produced a monocle, and is blithely trying to analyse the entrails of a plucked bird – via the cloaca.

Zarathustra: They have cold, dry eyes. Before them every bird flies unfeathered. This species of man boasts that they do not lie: but incapacity to lie is a long way from love of truth. Beware!

The Conscientious of Spirit looks up in surprise, dropping the monocle from his eye. The others return to their preparations.

Zarathustra: Freedom from fever is a long way from knowledge! I have no faith in thoroughly frozen spirits. He who cannot lie, does not know what truth is.

29 – Interior. Zarathustra's Cave. Evening

Zarathustra approaches the mule.

Zarathustra: If you would scale the heights, then use your own feet! Don't allow yourself to be carried. Don't settle yourself on the backs (*aside:*) – or brains – of others! So you mount your stead? (*mounts the mule*) You charge headlong to your lofty goal? Well then, my friends! (*stands-up on the mule's back*) But your lame foot is in the saddle with you! (*his foot slips, and he falls back astride the mule*) When you reach your goal; when you spring from your horse: there, precisely there at your peak, you Higher Men (*dismounts, and falls to his backside*) – you shall stumble!

30 – Interior. Zarathustra's Cave. Evening

Zarathustra looks to the Voluntary Beggar, who is trying to season his dish to the taste of the others, but finds it more-and-more unpalatable himself.

Zarathustra: You creators, you Higher Men! One is only ever pregnant with ones own child. Don't allow yourselves to become filled with objections! Objects fill your senses – neighbourly seductions! But who, then – who is your neighbour? – And so you live "for your neighbour" – still, it's not for him that you create! – Unlearn a this for-doing, I say, you creators: let it be precisely your virtue that you do nothing "for" or "because" or "since." Let your ears be waxed shut against such false little words. – "For your neighbour" – that is the virtue of little people. They say "like unto like" and "hand washes hand" – they have neither the power nor the right to what is good *for you*. In your *own* estimation of virtue, in your *self*-esteem, you creators, is the fore-knowledge and foreboding of – a pregnancy! That which no-one has yet laid eyes on – on the fruit – that's what your entire soul shields and shapes and nurtures. Where your entire soul is – with your children – there too is your entire virtue! Your work, your will – that is your neighbour, your nearest and dearest. Never allow false values to impose themselves upon you!

The Voluntary Beggar has re-created his dish to his own taste, and is beaming with satisfaction.

31 – Interior. Zarathustra's Cave. Evening

Zarathustra looks to the Enchanter, who is trying to impress the others with his capacity to juggle dishes and produce magical results of various sorts. At the crux of a very difficult trick, a key prop shatters, and the guests all stand with anxious expressions, as if in fear at the consequences of the shattered illusion.

Zarathustra (*with cheerful encouragement*)**:** The higher the type, the more seldom a thing fits the mould. You Higher Men – are you not all misfits and mould-breakers? But don't lose heart! What does it matter? How much is still possible! Learn to laugh at yourselves – over and beyond yourselves – as one must. You simply *have* to laugh! Little wonder that you miss the mark, you shattered souls – are you not marked men, one-and-all? Is it not in you that the future of mankind is welling-up and swelling-up? Mankind's most distant, deepest, most astronomical, most unfathomable powers – are they not all foaming in your cauldrons? What wonder, then, that many a kettle cracks! Learn to laugh at yourselves, as one must. You simply have to laugh, you Higher Men. – Oh how much is still possible! And truly, how much has already worked-out well! How rich is this Earth in good little perfect things, in happy outcomes! Surround yourselves with good little perfect things, you Higher Men! Their golden ripeness heals the heart. Perfection teaches hope (*pops a grape into his mouth*).

32 – Interior. Zarathustra's Cave. Evening

Zarathustra approaches another dish.

Zarathustra: What was here on Earth the greatest sin hitherto? Was it not the word of him who said "Woe unto those here who laugh!" Did he himself find no reason on Earth to laugh? Then he cannot have looked too close! (*leans over to inspect the ground*) Good grounds here for laughter (*he overbalances, somersaults, and lands on his bottom. Laughing:*) – is childsplay! – He had not enough love, else he had loved us laughers too! But he hated and baited us, putting us down as howlers and growlers (*portrays a bogey man*). But must one always curse where one has no love? That seems to me to be in bad taste. But that's what he did, that lover of the unconditional! (*sits in lotus position, palms outstretched, eyes closed, and head-turned, as if to "hear-no-evil, see-no-evil"*) He was at one – with the rabble. And he didn't love himself nearly enough either – else he had raged a little less that he was unloved. No great love seeks merely to be loved – great love has a higher goal. Stay out of the ways of such unconditional lovers! They – are a pathological, impoverished species – a sort of rabble. They look on this life badly, with an evil eye for this world, this Earth (*throws a handful of dust up over himself, squints through the cloud, then springs to his feet*). Stay out of the ways of such pedants and pettifoggers! They have heavy feet, and sullen hearts – they know not – to dance! (*clicks-up his heels*) How could such a species make light of the Earth!

Zarathustra kicks-up great clouds of dust as he begins a wild and impetuous dance.

33 – Interior. Zarathustra's Cave. Evening

Zarathustra (*still dancing*): All good things approach their goals with twists and turns. Like cats they arch their back (*does a back-flip*) and purr to themselves, humming the beeline to their happiness – it's nearby! And all good things laugh! Ones carriage betrays whether one is on ones own rails (*balances an apple on his head as he walks*). So look at me go! (*makes a run and tumble, leaping over the heads of the others, somersaulting, and landing on his feet*) He who is near his goal, however, he dances! And truly, I should have to be cast in stone, statuesque – (*poses like a statue, then aside:*) I wouldn't stand for it – a pillar, rigid, dumb – (*produces the stone of a plum between his teeth, which he spits out*) stonefaced – I love fast footwork. And even if there is morass and sorrow on Earth (*pours a libation*) – he who has light feet rises above the mire – with ease – and dances as if on polished ice (*does the splits, hurting himself, and gets up laughing*). Raise yourselves up, my brothers, high! Higher!

The guests rather stupidly and clumsily attempt various dancesteps or acrobatics. The scene is pure farce, and soon all are in fits at their own folly.

Zarathustra: ... And forget me not your feet! (*takes a swipe at the kings with his stock*) Raise your feet up too, you good dancers, and better still – stand on your heads!

Left tumbles head-over-heels into Right, knocking him over in similar fashion, and soon all are flat on their backsides, laughing and looking to Zarathustra.

34 – Interior. Zarathustra's Cave. Evening

A Chorus of birds enters and dances a roundelay about the cave, showering the guests with flowers and wreaths. Zarathustra takes a wreath of golden roses.

Zarathustra (*laughing*): This crown of laughter, this ring around the rosary – I hereby adorn myself with this crown. I hereby consecrate my own laughter. I have found no-one else – today – who's up to the task. Zarathustra the dancer – light as a feather – beckoning with wings ready-to-fly. Zarathustra – who flocks with the birds – set to soar, ominous (*takes a cooked chicken from the spit*) and done to perfection! – Zarathustra the soothsayer. Zarathustra the sooth-laugher. Never impatient. Never unconditional. One who loves leaps and side-springs – I adorn myself with this crown!

Zarathustra deftly flips the wreath onto his head, where it sits like a crown.

35 – Interior. Zarathustra's Cave. Evening

All are now merrily beginning to share in the spirit of the occasion.

Zarathustra (*comically illustrates each thought with a prank*): Raise up your hearts, my brothers! High! Higher! And forget me not your feet! Raise up your feet too, you good dancers, and better still – stand on your heads! Even in happiness there are ponderous beasts. Some are flat-footed from go to whoa; amazingly they work themselves up, like an elephant straining to stand on its head. But better the fool that jumps for joy, than the fool that slumps in sorrow – better to dance clumsy than to walk lame. Thus my wisdom has taught me – (*aside:*) down pat –: Even the worst thing has two good flip-sides. Even the worst thing has two good dance-shoes. So learn to teach yourselves, you Higher Men, to stand on your own two feet! – For mine, then, unlearn all this moping and doping, all this sighing and crying – and this wailing of the mournfu mob! Oh how these sad-sacks make it hard in the human race. Today, however, the rabble are in the lead.

36 – Interior. Zarathustra's Cave. Evening

The scene becomes a symphony of flatulence.

Zarathustra: For mine, one should be like the wind as it blasts from its mountain caves –

A fart is heard.

Zarathustra: – it seeks to dance to its own tune, the seas shake and roll to the tap of its feet.

Several small farts sound out.

Zarathustra: He gives the mule wings, he milks the lioness. Praised be this benevolent unbounded spirit, who comes to every dog and every day – like a stormwind –

A long, loud fart sounds out.

Zarathustra: – enemy to the heads of thistles and thinkers, and to all wilting leaves and weeds. Praised be this wild huntsman and good free spirit of the storm –

Zarathustra listens, but no fart is heard.

Zarathustra: – who dances over morass and sorrow as over fields of flowers! You Higher Men, your worst is that you have not yet learned to dance as one *has* to dance – to dance over and beyond yourselves, and away! What does it matter that you are turned-out all wrong! How much is still possible! So learn, then, to laugh over and beyond yourselves – and away! (*in making a grand gesture, stumbles awkwardly. laughs at himself*) Raise up your hearts, you good dancers – High! Higher!

The two worst dancers – the Conscientious of Spirit and Ugliest Man – have left-off the feast to follow Zarathustra's call, as though he were calling a dance.

Zarathustra (*doubling-over in fits*): And forget me not some hearty laughter too!

All are in fits of laughter.

Zarathustra (*taking the wreath from his head*): This crown of laughter, this ring around the rosary – with you, my brothers, I close-out this round. To you I pass the crown!

Zarathustra tosses the wreath over his shoulder, like a bride. The guests, vying for the wreath, fall in a heap on the ground.

Zarathustra (*recovering his composure, teary-eyed*): I have pronounced laughter sacred, you Higher Men. Learn, I say – learn to laugh!

The guests are left rolling on the ground, as if exhausted.

37 – Exterior. Zarathustra's Cave. Night

Zarathustra, slips-out from the entrance to the cave.

Zarathustra: Ah, wholesome air all about me! Ah, blessed quiet! But where are my animals? Come! Come here, my Eagle, my Serpent!

Eagle and Serpent appear and sit with Zarathustra.

Zarathustra: Tell me now, my animals: These Higher Men one-and-all – do they perhaps – not smell so good? – – Oh wholesome fragrance all about me! Now I feel how much – and know why – I love you, my animals.

Eagle, Serpent and Zarathustra huddle together and breathe deep.

38 – Interior. Zarathustra's Cave. Night

Enchanter gets to his feet, and looks slyly about.

Enchanter: He's gone out! Again already, you Higher Men – to tickle your fancies with this term of praise and flattery, like he himself – already my trickster-spirit and magic daemon sits upon me, my heavy-hearted devil – to whom this Zarathustra is fundamentally opposed.

A satyr has begun to dance, solo, in the shadows.

Enchanter: Forgive it him! It is his will, now, to appear before your very eyes. This is precisely his time of the night. I wrestle with this evil spirit – in vain. To you all – to you who should like to do yourselves verbal honours, whether you call yourselves "the free spirits" or "the truthful" or "the Penitents of the Spirit" or "the liberated" or "the Yearners of the Great Yearning" – to you all, to you who – like me – suffer at the Great Nausea, since the old God died and no new god yet weighs in the cradle – to you alone is my evil spirit and magic devil precious. I know you, you Higher Men – I know him. I know also this bootless friend Zarathustra, whom I love against my will. He himself, it often seems to me, resembles a beautiful, saintly shroud and cloistered cover-up. Like some amazing, newfangled holy hood-winkle, in which my evil spirit – the heavy-hearted devil – rejoices. I love Zarathustra, I often think, because my evil spirit will have it so!

A maenad has joined the satyr in the shadow dance.

Enchanter: But he falls upon me again now, and compels me, this spirit of melancholy, this twilight-of-the-evening's devil – and truly, you Higher Men, it is his lust – just open your eyes! – it is his most passionate desire to come naked, whether male or female, I never know. But he comes, he compels me – Woe! Open up your senses.

The satyr and maenad emerge from the shadows, dancing an extremely sensual, suggestive, and erotic ballet.

Enchanter (*takes up his lyre and begins to tune it as he speaks*)**:** The day fades away. The evening comes to all things now – even to the best of things. So listen and see, you Higher Men, just what sort of devil – whether man- or she-devil – this Spirit-of-the-Evening Melancholy is!

39 – Interior. Zarathustra's Cave. Night

Enchanter strums the lyre and sings. The ballet is gradually joined by a full chorus of satyrs and maenads, and illustrates every sensual connotation of the lyrics.

Enchanter: In cleared-up air,

The Song of Melancholy

when the soothing dew-drop
has already flowed to earth,
unseen, unheard too –
for the soothing dew-drop – as do all tender mercies –
comes on feathered feet:
Did you think then, did you think, Glowing Heart,
how once you thirsted
after heavenly tears and trickles of dew –
how parched and weary you thirsted,
while malicious eventide beams-of-sunshine,
on tracks of golden grass,
ran blinding rings around you,
winking with joy in your discomfort
through black trees.

"The suitor of *Truth*? You? – thus they mocked –
No! only a poet!
A beast –
(*makes three distinctive gestures*)
a cunning, thieving, creeping,
deceiving beast
that knowingly, willingly has to lie
Lusting for prey with motley maskings –
A mask himself, prey himself –
Is *that* – the Suitor of Truth?
No! Only a fool! Only a poet!
Only motley bluster,
motley waffle from painted fools,
climbing motley rainbows,
on spans of words, lying
between false heavens
and false Earths – drifting, flitting –
Only a fool! *Only* a poet!

Is *that* – the suitor of Truth?
Not calm, cold, clear, crystal,
Built to the image, to the Pillar of God –
not stood before temples,
a god's sentinel:
No! Hostile to such statues-of-truth,
More at home in every wilderness

than before temples –
Full of feline mischief,
jumping through every window – Swish!
Sniffing around at every chance,
in every jungle – sniffing
wistfully-addicted,
to running through jungles
with mottle-flecked beasts
– sinfully sound and motley beautiful.
You run with lustful lips,
blissfully mocking, blissfully Hellish, blissfully bloodlustful,
(*repeats the distinctive gestures*)
rapacious, stalking, deceiving –

Or like the eagle that stares and stares
Entranced, into abysmal depths –
Into *his* abysses –
– oh how he circles, around and around,
downwards, inwards, waywards!
Then suddenly
– like an arrow –
wings drawn,
lunging for little lambs,
hurtling down, hungry-eyed,
lusting for lambflesh,
with malice for the souls of sheep,
grimly set against all that looks sheepish,
lamb-eyed, warm-and-fuzzy,
or pale, with the cozenous cosy goodwill of the flocking flock!

Thus – like an eagle, like a panther,
are the yearnings of the poets.
Thus are *your* yearnings behind the thousand masks,
You fool! You poet!

You, who looked upon man,
and saw God as a sheep –
and the god *torn to pieces* in man,
like the sheep in man,
and torn apart *laughing* –

That, *that* is thy bliss!
A heaven for panthers and eagles!
A heaven for poets and fools! –

In cleared-up air,
when already the sickle of the moon, green
stalks enviously through the crimsons of the sky –
opposed to the day,
secretive with every step,
slashing at rosen hammocks,
until they sink – slunken down
into the colourless night –

Thus I sank one time myself,
away from my delusions of Truth,
away from my yearnings of the day –
weary of the day, sickened by the light –
I sank downwards, evening-wards, shadow-wards –
scorched by a truth and thirsting –
Did you think then, did you think, Glowing Heart,
How thus you thirsted?
That from all Truth
I am forbidden –
Only a fool! Only a poet!

40 – Interior. Zarathustra's Cave. Night

All except the Conscientious of Spirit are about to join-in the ballet.

Conscientious of Spirit (*snatches the lyre from the Enchanter*): Air! Let's have some fresh air in here! Let Zarathustra back in! You make this cave torrid and toxic, you shoddy old charlatan! You seduce, you enchant, you finesse, to unconscious desires and unknown wildernesses – and woe, when such as you make presentations – and representations – of the truth! Woe unto all free spirits who're not on the look-out for such enchanters! It's all over with their freedom – you hoax and coax – back into confinement! You old melancholy devil – the piper's call beckons from your lament! Such as you praise chastity – as a secret invitation to the pots-of-flesh!

Enchanter (*looks around and sees that the others are all still firmly under his spell*): Quiet! Good songs require time to reverb. After a good song one ought to have long silence. That's what these, these Higher Men one-and-all are doing. You, however, have perhaps not understood much of my song? There is little magic spirit in you, I should say.

Conscientious of Spirit: You praise me inasmuch you distinguish me from yourself! Well then! But you others, what do I see? You all sit here still, with lecherous eyes. You free souls, where is your freedom! Almost, it seems to me, you're like such as have been staring at wicked young girls dancing about naked – your souls themselves dance! In you, you Higher Men, there must be more of what the Enchanter calls his evil spirit of magic and deception – we must certainly be different. And truly, we spoke and thought enough amongst ourselves before Zarathustra came home to this cave, so it's not as if I didn't know – we *are* different. We seek different things, too, up here, you and I. I – to be exact – seek more *security.* That's why I came to Zarathustra. He, to be exact, is the steadiest tower – his, the most steadfast will today. Today – where everything wavers, where the whole Earth is quaking. You, however, when I look and see the eyes that you make – I almost think you to be in search of more *insecurity* – more horror, more danger, more earthquakes. It almost seems to me that you're in lust – forgive my presumption, you Higher Men – that you're in lust after the most desperate, dangerous lives. Lives that to me promise the most fear. The lives of wild beasts, of jungles, caverns, steep mountains and gaping pitfalls of error. And it's not the one who can lead you *out* of danger who pleases you best, but the one who misleads you, who seduces you to abandon every pathway. But if such cravings on your part were *real*, it seems to me nevertheless *impossible.* Fear, namely, is humanity's defining inheritance, its fundamental instinct. Through fear one comes to account for everything – for original-sin and inherent-virtue alike. From fear *my* virtue, too, has grown – namely Science. The fear – to be precise – of wild beasts – whose taming has for the longest time been part of human cultivation – until finally it has come to the beast one hides within – and fears most. Zarathustra calls it "the Inner Cow." Such a long-lived ancient fear, ultimately wrought to a fine art, ghostly, delicate, spiritual – today, it seems to me, it has come to be called *Science*...

41 – Interior. Zarathustra's Cave. Night

Zarathustra has returned unnoticed and overheard the last speech. He hands the Conscientious of Spirit a handful of roses, and laughs.

Zarathustra: What! What's this I hear? Verily, methinks, either thou art a fool, or I am one myself. And now I will stand your "truth" – Hey Presto! (*launches forward into a hand-stand and somersault*) – on its head: Fear, to be precise – is our exception. Courage, however, and adventure, and pleasure in the unknown and unexpected – *Courage*, it seems to me, is the entire prehistory of mankind. From the wildest animals man has first coveted, and then appropriated every last virtue. Thus in the first instance did he become – human. This courage, ultimately wrought to a fine art – spirited, spiritual – this human-heart with eagles' wings and a serpent's cunning – this, it seems to me, is called today...

The guests interrupt with a chorus of "Zarathustra!" *– then all laugh, as if relieved of their various burdens.*

Enchanter: Well now! He's gone, my evil spirit! And did I not warn you of him myself, when I said that he was a deceiver, a spirit both magic and tragic? Especially – to say it aloud – when he comes from behind. But what can I help it for his tricks! Did I create him and the world? Well then! Let us be all well again, and of good cheer! And although Zarathustra casts an evil eye – look at him – he's angry with me – before night comes he will learn to love and praise me again. He cannot live long without committing such little follies. He – loves his enemies – he understands this artform better than anyone I've ever seen. But he takes-out revenge for it – on his friends!

The guests applaud the Enchanter. Zarathustra does a round of handshakes, as if in atonement, but with his usual playful mixture of sincerity and malice, until, by the entrance to the cave, he is tempted to duck out again.

42 – Interior. Zarathustra's Cave. Night

Shadow: Don't go out! Stay with us – lest that dank old despondency falls upon us again. The old Enchanter has already given us the best of his worst, and behold! the good, pious Pope there had tears in his eyes, and had completely set sail again on a sea of melancholy. These kings here may well be putting on a brave face in front of us – that's the best lesson they've learnt of us all today. But if there were no-one to witness, I wager, even with them the evil hour would begin again. The evil hour of drawing clouds, of dank melancholy, of falling skies, of stolen sunshine, of howling autumn wind – the evil hour of our howling and cries of distress. Stay with us, O Zarathustra! There is much hidden misery here – that wants to speak. Much eventide, much cloud, much heavy air! You nourish us with robust man-food and powerful sayings. Don't clear the way, now, for another serving of that enfeebling female spirit as our dessert! You alone make the air about you strong and clear! Have I ever on Earth anywhere found such good air as here with you in your cave? And I've seen many lands. My nose is trained to prove – or disprove – a variety of airs. But with you my nostrils catch their greatest pleasure! Unless it were – lest it were – ah, forgive an old recollection! Forgive me an old supper-song that I once composed among the daughters of the Wilderness – by whom, to be exact, there is a similar good clear tropical air (*picks up the lyre, and tunes it a little as he speaks*). There, where I was furthest from the cloudy dank melancholy of "Cultural Capitals"! Then, when love – to me – was a sort of girl from the East – a kind of sky-blue kingdom-of-heaven – over which there hung no cloud, nor thought. You wouldn't believe how well they sat with me – when they weren't dancing – deep, but without a thought, like sweet-nothings, like little secrets, like peas in a nutshell, like riddles to be unwrapped after a meal – motley and strange, to be sure, but without a cloud – riddles, but not without a clue. For the love of such girls I once proposed this after-dinner – psalm (*strums the lyre and begins to sing*). The wilderness grows. Woe unto them that hide hidden wildernesses!

43 – Interior. Zarathustra's Cave. Night

A satyr is at the feet of a chorus of maenads in grass skirts, lighted so as to be visible from the waist down only.

Shadow (*singing*): Ha! Splendid!
        Splendid indeed!
        A worthy beginning!
        Splendidly exotic!
        Worthy of a lion
    – or a screeching moral-monkey –
        but nothing for you,
You, my most adorable young lady-friends,
        at whose feet
        – for the first time –
        it is granted me to sit,
    a cultured stiff among the palms. Sela.

        Wonderful indeed!
        Here I now sit
    – hard by the wilderness, and yet
    again so far from the wilderness –
    and bewildered by Nothingness too.
        Namely, swallowed down whole
        by this tiniest oasis.
        She spread herself wide,
        her lovely jaws gaping –
    the most fragrant of all little mouths –
        then I fell on in,
    down there, through that – amongst you,
You, my most adorable young lady-friends! Sela.

The Maenads begin a slow-paced belly dance.

Shadow: All hail! Hail to that whale
    if he left his guest feeling half-as-good –
    you get my learnéd innuendo?
    All hail to his belly
    if it was an oasis-belly
like one of these – and I call it into question –
    for I hail from the Land of Culture,
    and she is more fond of finding doubt
than all the tattletaling old-wives all tolled –
    God love her! Amen.

    So here I sit,
    in this tiniest oasis,
    like a date –
brazen, bronzed-up, laden with syrup, lusting
    for a maidens fulsome mouth –
but still more for the bite of cutting, snow-white, ice-cold
    girlish teeth (*aside:*) – that's what all hot dates
    drool at the mouth for. Sela.

Shadow is picked up by the satyr and drawn passively into the dance.

Shadow: Like the aforesaid fruit of southern parts
    – all-too-like-it –
    I lie here
    flapped and flicked about
    by the wings of little lady birds,
    and just the same by still smaller,
    more foolish and more sinful
    wishes and inclinations –
    bed-bugged all about by you,
    you unspeaking female felines,
    full of foreboding
    – Dudu and Suleika.
    Sphinxed about – if in a single word
    I may stuff such a fund of feelings –
    (*aside:*) God forgive me
    this sin against the word Itself! –
Sitting here, quaffing the very best of air,
    the air of Paradise indeed –
air as light as Light itself, with golden stripes.

Grass skirts are whirling all about him.

> Such fine air as only ever fell before
> – from the moon.
> Be it by accident,
> or is it come about by some excess of high spirits?
> – as the ancient poets put it.

The guests are riveted by the show, and are drinking freely.

Shadow (*becoming tipsy*): I however, call it into question
> – doubter that I am.
> For I hail from the Land of Culture,
> and she is more fond of finding doubt
> than all the tattletaling old-wives all tolled –
> God love her!
> Amen.

> Drinking this most splendiferous air
> with nostrils flared-out like flagons,
> with no future, with no memories,
> so here I sit, you
> my most adorable young lady-friends –
> and watch the palms,
> how they – like a dancing girl
> bend and sway and rub from side-to-side –
> it's mesmerizing!

The other guests are all still seated, a little tipsy, and swaying in time with the gyrations of the dancing maenads.

Shadow (*increasingly tipsy*): Like a dancing girl, who
> – it would seem to me –
> far too long already – dangerously long –
> is stood ever and anon on a single leg?

The Shadow is crawling about comically while the First Maenad balances gracefully and pirouettes on a single leg. The routine is comic-slapstick-ballet, laden with innuendo.

Shadow: Has she not then forgotten – it would seem to me –
> the other leg? In vain, at least
> I sought the missing jewel to the pair –
> the other leg, that is –

in the sacred vicintity of her most adorable,
most thoroughly exquisite
flitting and flapping, flashing – sashing.
Yes, you beautiful young lady-friends,
if you will believe me at all –
She's lost it!
It's gone!
Gone forever!
The other leg!
Oh what a shame about that other lovely leg!
Where – could it be waiting, mourning and forsaken?
A leg alone?
In fear, perhaps,
of some wild, shaggy, blond-headed
beast of a lion? Or even
already nibbled away, gnawed away –
Oh pitiful! Oh woe! Gnawed away! Sela.

Oh cry not for me,
Pale Heart!
Cry not for me,
ye of swaying heart and milky breast!
You little sack of sweet-heart-wood.

Satrys and maenads are writhing in an orgy of masturbation.

Shadow: Cry no more, pale Dudu!
Be a man, Suleika! Courage! Be brave!
– for perhaps something encouraging,
something heartening is at home in precisely this?
An anointed proverb?
A popular saying?

Ha! Up, Dignity!
Dignity of Virtue! Cultured dignity!
Up! Huff and puff again,
You bellows of virtue! Ha!
Roar one time more –
Roar with moral indignation!
Roar like a moral lion-of-virtue
roaring-up before the Daughters of the Wilderness!

For the howling of Virtue –
you most adorable young ladies –
is more than all cultured passion, cultured – craving!
And here I stand before you,
A Man of Culture,
I can do no other, so help me God!
Amen!

The Guests (*in solemn chorus*): The wilderness grows. Woe unto them that harbour wildernesses!

The guests – the mule included – fall amongst themselves laughing, and the scene is one of general merriment, and ease.

44 – Exterior. Zarathustra's Cave. Night

Zarathustra has slipped-out of the cave, and overhearing the sounds of merriment coming from within, he speaks, as if to his eagle and serpent.

Zarathustra: Where is their distress now? (*breathes deep*) Here with me, so it seems, they have unlearned their crying for help!

Guffaws of laughter, mixed with happy cries of Ye-ah from the Mule, resound from the cave.

Zarathustra: – if not, sadly, crying out altogether. (*listens again*) They're happy, and who knows? perhaps at their host's expense? Yet, even if they learned to laugh from me, it's still not *my* laughter they've learnt. But what does it matter? They're old, and convalesce in their own way. They laugh in their own way. My ears have suffered worse before now without turning dumb (*pauses to reflect*). This day is a victory, and it will soon fade. He flies, you know, the Spirit-of-Gravity – my old arch-enemy! How well this day will end, that so gravely and badly began! – And end it will! Evening is here already. He rides the waves – and well with me! How he rocks in his purple saddle! Returning home, blessed (*looks up at the stars in the sky*). Tis clear, the heavens look too. The world lies deep. O all you amazing men – having come to me – with me, life is worthwhile!

Another round of laughter sounds from the cave.

Zarathustra: They're taking the bait. My lure's working. It fades for them too, their enemy, the Spirit-of-Gravity – if my ears don't deceive me. They're beginning to learn how to laugh above and beyond themselves. My man-food's working – my proverbial vigour-and-vim – and verily, I didn't merely feed them up on flatulents! It was food fit for warriors and conquerors – I have awoken new curiosities. New hopes are in their arms and legs. Their hearts stretch forth. They find new words. Soon, their spirit will breathe – courage itself. Such food is certainly not fit for children, nor for sentimental young and little-old women either. One persuades their inner-workings in other ways. Their physician and teacher I am not (*pauses to reflect*). Their nausea fades from these Higher Men. Well then! that is my victory. In my domain, they are safe. All stupid shame flees from them. They're opening up. They're opening up their hearts. Good times are coming back to them. They're commemorating and ruminating again. They have become grateful. That I take as the best of signs. They have become grateful. Not long now and they will think themselves up – and up to festivals: erecting memorials to the enjoyment of times gone by. They are convalescents!

The ruckus from the cave dies-out completely. Zarathustra pricks-up his ears and lifts his nose, as if smelling something.

Zarathustra: What's happening? What are they up to?

He slinks stealthily to the entrance, and peeks in.

45 – Interior. Zarathustra's Cave. Night

The guests are all on their knees, as if in worship before the Mule. Some pine-cones have been kindled into a little fire, as incense.

Zarathustra: They have all become pious again. They're praying! They're insane!
Ugliest Man (*coughs phlegmatically, then breaks into a pious litany directed at the Mule*)**:** Amen! And praise and honour and wisdom

and thanks and glory and strength be unto our God, from Eternity to Eternity!
Mule: Ye-ah!
Ugliest Man: He carries our burdens. He takes-on the shape of a worker. He is patient from the heart, and never says No! And whoever loves his God spares him not – the rod.
Mule: Ye-ah!
Ugliest Man: He never speaks, lest it be to say "Ye-ah!" to the world he created – thus he praises his world. It is his cunning that he never speaks – thus he is seldom in the wrong.
Mule: Ye-ah!
Ugliest Man: He passes unnoticed through the world. Grey is the colour of his coat – in it he hides his virtue. If he has spirit, he conceals it – everyone, however, believes in his long ears.
Mule: Ye-ah!
Ugliest Man: What hidden wisdom it is that he sports long ears and says only Yeah, and never Nay! Has he not created the world after his own image – namely, as stupid as possible?
Mule: Ye-ah!
Ugliest Man: Thou goest straight and crooked ways. It bothers thee little what mankind think to be straight or crooked. Beyond good and evil is thy kingdom. It is thy innocence not to know what innocence is.
Mule: Ye-ah!
Ugliest Man: And behold! You push no-one away – the beggars nor the kings. You suffer the little children to come to you. And when the wicked knaves tease you, you simply say Ye-ah!
Mule: Ye-ah!
Ugliest Man: You love she-asses and fresh figs. You are not one to fast. A thistle tickles your heart when you're hungry. Therein lies the wisdom of a god.
Mule: Ye-ah!

46 – Interior. Zarathustra's Cave. Night

Zarathustra springs into the midst of his guests.

Zarathustra: Ye-ah! What are you doing here, you sons-of-men? Woe, if anyone but Zarathustra saw what you're up to (*does a round of the cave, picking his guests up from the ground*). You'd stand condemned – with your newfound belief – of being the worst of blasphemers – or the most foolish of little-old women! And you yourself, you old Pope: How does it sit with you, that you sit here and add your voice to the worship of God in the shape of an ass?
Old Pope: O Zarathustra, forgive me, but in matters of God I am more enlightened even than you. And so it's quite proper – better to worship God like this, in this shape, than in no shape at all! Think this saying over, my exulted friend – you will speedily come to appreciate that there is wisdom hidden somewhere in there. He who said "God is a spirit" – he made the greatest leap yet-on-Earth towards disbelief. Such a saying is not-on-Earth easily made good! My old heart leapt and lifted when there came to be again something-on-Earth to worship. Forgive me that, O Zarathustra – from the heart of a pious old Pope.
Zarathustra (*to the Shadow*)**:** And you – you spiel and deal yourself up to be a free spirit? Yet you serve yourself up here to the worship of idols? You serve yourself worse, here – you sorry new convert – than you did with your wild and wicked maidens!
Shadow: Bad enough, you're right. But what can I help it! The old God lives again, O Zarathustra, you can say what you will. The Ugliest Man is to blame for it all, he resurrected him. And even though he said he had once killed him – *death is, with gods, never anything but a prejudice.*
Zarathustra: And you, you sorry old magician – what have you done! Who – in these liberated times – is going to believe in you, when you believe in such asinine gods? It has been pure folly to do such a thing. How could you, as clever as you are – How could you be so foolish!
Enchanter: O Zarathustra, you're right – it was foolishness. It weighs hard upon me already.
Zarathustra (*to the Conscientious of Spirit*)**:** And even you! Weigh it up, and lay a finger aside of your nose! Does nothing here go against your conscience? Is your spirit not too clean for all this praying, and the humours of these bedfellows?

A long, protracted fart echoes around the cave.

Conscientious of Spirit: There is something in it (*lays his finger aside of his nose, and bows his head, as if to consider*) – there is something in this playacting that clears my conscience (*breathes deep*). Perhaps that I cannot believe in God, except that God in this shape is surely the most believable of all. God ought to be eternal, according to all the most pious of testimony. Whoever had so much time, would take his time – as slow and stupid as possible. He could do so much with it! And whoever had too much spirit might well befuddle himself in folly and foolishness. Think of yourself, O Zarathustra! You yourself – truly! You too could become an ass from excess and wisdom. Does a consummate sage not go happily down the most intractable pathways? By all appearances they do, O Zarathustra – by your appearance!

Zarathustra (*turns to the Ugliest Man, who is still on the ground, reaching up to offer the Mule a wineskin*): And finally you, you unspeakable thing – What have you done! You seem to be changed. There's a gleam in your eye. The mantle of the sublime cloaks your ugliness. What is it that's happened here? Is it true then – what the others are saying – that you've resurrected him again? And for what? Was he not put to death and abolished on good grounds? You yourself seem to me resurrected. What have you done? How have you changed so? Why have you converted yourself? Speak, you unspeakable thing!

Ugliest Man: O Zarathustra, you are a scoundrel! Whether he yet lives, or lives again, or is thoroughly dead – which of us two knows that best, I ask you? But one thing I do know – I learnt it once from you yourself, O Zarathustra – whoever wants to kill most thoroughly – he laughs. Not with anger, but with laughter – one conjures death, one dies – laughing! With laughter – thus you once pronounced it – O Zarathustra, you obscurantist, you gay reaper, you dangerous saint, you – are a scoundrel!

47 – Interior. Zarathustra's Cave. Night

Zarathustra springs back to the entrance, then turns to face his guests.

Zarathustra (*in a loud voice*): O you buffoons, you knaves-fools one-and-all! How you make believe and hide yourselves from me! How in every one of you your hearts skipped with mischief and delight, as if it were that you had finally become as little children again, namely pious – that again you finally came to do as children do, namely to pray, to clasp your hands and say "dear God"! But for mine you must leave, now, this kindergarten – my own cave – which is home, today, to all sorts of childishness. Come outside and cool your childish impetuousness – cool your hot-headed, hot-hearted hot blood down! Granted: Lest ye not become as little children, ye shall never come into the kingdom of heaven (*motions upwards*). But we don't even want to go to heaven! We are become as men: Thus we seek – the kingdom of Earth.

There is a long silence as Zarathustra gazes at the guests – all still very cheery – one-by-one, as they ponder his words.

48 – Interior. Zarathustra's Cave. Night

Zarathustra's face seems transformed.

Zarathustra: O my new friends, you wonders amongst wonders, you Higher Men, how well you please me now –

Zarathustra beckons to the guests to come to him.

Zarathustra (*warmly*):
– since you have become cheerful again! You have all verily blossomed. To tell the truth, I think such flowers as you to have need of new festivals – a little mettlesome nonsense, some or other braying and praying, a celebration and service to God or Mule – some sort of fata-Zarathustra: a mistral, a cool breeze to clear the doldrums of your souls.

The guests file one-by-one past Zarathustra as he speaks.

The Song of Intoxication

Zarathustra: Never forget this night, nor this Assfest, you Higher Men! *That's* what you discovered here with me, and that's something I take to be a good omen – such things are only ever discovered by convalescents! And if you celebrate it ever again – this Assfest – do it to honour yourselves. Do it to honour me too! And to memory of me!

Ugliest Man is the last to leave the cave.

49 – Exterior. Zarathustra's Cave. Night

Zarathustra has taken the Ugliest Man by the hand, and shows her the full moon and the sparkling fountain a little way across from the cave. All seem refreshed and somewhat in awe of the beautiful night. Zarathustra beams, like a proud father.

Ugliest Man (*looking rather beautiful in the moonlight, clears her throat, then speaks in a clean, clear voice, as never before*): My friends one-and-all, what do you think? For the sake of this day – I am, for the first time, happy to have lived my whole life. And though I affirm so much, it seems to me not nearly enough. Life here on Earth *is* worthwhile. One day, one feast with Zarathustra has taught me to love the Earth. "Was *that* life?" I will say unto Death – "Well then! Once more!" – My friends, what do you think? Won't you say with me unto Death "Was *that* life? For the sake of Zarathustra – Well then! Once more!"

The guests all suddenly become aware of heir own transformation and newfound health – and of their gratitude. They fall upon Zarathustra, some laughing, some crying, some kissing his hand. The Old Prophet dances with joy. He is joined by, at first one, then an entire chorus of Maenads. All stop and stare, however, when the Mule – as if inspired – begins to dance too.

50 – Exterior. Zarathustra's Cave. Midnight

The Mule dances a solo, and Zarathustra swoons, as if drunk. He lies limp in the arms of the guests as the Mule and his Soul dance, pas de deux, the coniunctio. Coming to himself, but still somewhat intoxicated by events, Zarathustra puts his finger to his lips, and listens. A distant bell tolls the first stroke of midnight.

Zarathustra (*in a faint voice*): Come! (*listens again, then speaks with newfound voice*) Come! Come! Midnight approaches! Come! Let us a take a turn! This is the hour. Let us a take a turn in the night!

Bell tolls again.

51 – Exterior. Zarathustra's Cave. Midnight

The guests all stroll with Zarathustra as he rhapsodizes. His words are a narrative to the danse macabre of the maenads, who are whisked away, one-by-one, by a chorus of satyrs, who remain.

Zarathustra: You Higher Men, midnight is come – thus will I whisper a little something in your ear, just as yon old bell whispers in mine – so strange, so terrifying, so profound. Just as yon midnight bell tells it to me, having lived through more than any man, having tolled many times already – the profoundest agonies of your fathers. Ah! Oh! How she sighs! How she laughs in her reverie! – that profound, ancient midnight of old! Hush! Hush! Here one hears much that sounds as silence to the day. But now, in the cool air, where even the rushing of your blood is stilled – now it speaks, now it is heard, now it creeps into nocturnally oversightful souls. Ah! Oh! How she sighs! How she laughs in her dream! Do you not hear how strange, how frighteningly she speaks to you – that deep, deep, ancient midnight!

Chorus of Satyrs: O Mankind, attend!

The dance has run its course, and Zarathustra's Soul, alone of the maenads, remains. The bell tolls again.

52 – Exterior. Zarathustra's Cave. Midnight

Zarathustra: Oh me! Where has the time flown? Am I not sunk in deep fountains? The world sleeps. Ah! Oh! The wolf howls. The moon shines. Sooner shall I die, to die sooner than tell you what lies in my heart by midnight deep. Now I die –

Zarathustra's Soul is lifted, as on a bier, by a cortège of satyrs.

Zarathustra: It is gone. Spider, what's that you spin around me? Is it blood you want? Ah! Oh! The dew falls. The hour has come – the hour where I am wedded and webbed, where I freeze; the hour that asks and asks –
Zarathustra and First Satyr: "Who has heart enough for it?"
Two Satyrs: "Who shall master the Earth?"
Zarathustra: Who is it will say –
Chorus of Satyrs: "Thus shall you run, you streams great and small!"
Zarathustra: The time approacheth, O Man, thou – you Higher Man – attend! This is advice for superfine ears – for *thine* ears.
Zarathustra and the Satyrs: What says the deepest midnight deep?

Bell tolls again.

53 – Exterior. Zarathustra's Cave. Midnight

Zarathustra: It carries me away, my soul dances.

Zarathustra's Soul remains still. The guests look at each other with a confusion reflected in the whirr of colour and dance of the satyrs.

Zarathustra: Six feet of earth is the work of a day! Who shall be her master? The moon is cool. The wind falls quiet. Ah! Oh! Have you now flown high enough? You dance, but a leg is not yet a wing. Everything of pleasure, you good dancers, is now gone. Wine turns to grume. Every cup becomes brittle. The graves stammer. You flew not high enough – now the graves stammer.
First Satyr: "Redeem, now, the Dead!"

The maenads whirl back onto the stage, blending into the wild ballet of the satyrs.

Chorus of Satyrs: Why so long, Night?
First Satyr: "Does the moon not make us drunk?"
Zarathustra: You Higher Men, redeem now the graves! Awaken the corpses! Ah, the worm turns – How now? Handy Dandy! It is near. The hour is nigh. There's a rumbling of the bell. There's a snorting of the heart. There's a turning yet – of the woodworm, of the heartsworm. Ah! Oh!
Chorus of Maenads, Satyrs, and Zarathustra: The world is deep!

Bell tolls again.

54 – Exterior. Zarathustra's Cave. Midnight

Zarathustra (*in raptures*): Sweet lyre! Sweet lyre! I love thy tune, thy drunken slater-ball, see-no-evil tune! From how long, from how far has your tune come to me! Far indeed – from the ponds of love! You old bell. You sweet lyre! Every pain rends thee at heart – father's pain, forefather's pain! Thy council's become ripe – ripe, like golden autumn and afternoon, like the heart of a hermit. Now you speak. The world itself becomes ripe. The grapes turn. Now they will die – die of happiness. You Higher Men, do you not smell it? An uncanny scent fills the air – a mist and air of Eternity. A rosy-bronze gold-wine air of age-old happiness – of drunken dead-lucky midnight. It sings –
Chorus of Maenads, Satyrs, and Zarathustra: "The world is deep – and deeper than the day divined."

Bell tolls again.

55 – Exterior. Zarathustra's Cave. Midnight

Zarathustra (*in raptures*): Leave me! Leave me! I am too pure for thee. Rest not upon me! Has my world not just become perfect? My skin is too pure for thy hands.

The Song of Intoxication

The guests misunderstand Zarathustra's words, and back-off until he continues.

Zarathustra (*in raptures*): Leave me, you stupid, foolish day! Is the midnight not clearer? The purest shall be lords of the Earth – the most unrecognized, strongest; those of midnight-soul – cleverer and deeper than any day. O Day, you feel for me? You grope for my happiness? To thee, I am rich – a one-off, a treasure-chest, a gold-mine? O World, am I thy will? Am I worldly to thee? Am I spiritual to thee? Yet day and world – you are too clumsy. Get cleverer hands! Reach for deeper fortune – for deeper misfortune! Reach for a god, don't reach for me! My misfortune, my good fortune is deep, you wondrous Day – but I am no god, no god's Hell.
Chorus of Maenads, Satyrs, and Zarathustra: Deep is her woe.

Bell tolls again.

56 – Exterior. Zarathustra's Cave. Midnight

Zarathustra (*in raptures*): God's woe is deeper, you wondrous world! Reach for God's woe, not for me! What am I, but a sweet, drunken lyre – a midnight-lyre, a tolling doomsayer. No-one divines me. I have to speak – to the deaf, you Higher Men! For I see you do not understand. Thither! There! O Youth! O Midday! O Afternoon! Now evening and night and midnight are come. The hound bays. The wind – is the wind not a hound? It whimpers, whines, it howls. Ah! Oh! Midnight – how she sighs! How she laughs! How she moans and groans! Yet how soberly she speaks, this drunken poetess! She has perhaps drunk herself sober? She's become over-awake? Mulling herself over again? She brings her woe back up again, in a dream – the old, deep midnight deep. And her pleasure even more. For pleasure – if woe is deep –
Chorus of Maenads, Satyrs, and Zarathustra: Pleasure is deeper still than misery.

Bell tolls again.

57 – Exterior. Zarathustra's Cave. Midnight

Zarathustra (*in raptures*): You grapevine! How you praise me! Yet I cut you! I am cruel. You bleed – what does your praise want of my drunken cruelty? Thus you said it –
Chorus of Maenads, Satyrs, and Zarathustra: "All that becomes perfect – everything ripe – sets itself upon death!"
Zarathustra: Blesséd, blesséd be the vintner's knife! Yet all that is unripe is set upon life! Woe unto thee! Woe says –
Chorus of Maenads, Satyrs, and Zarathustra: "Pass on! Away with thee! Oh, woe is me!"
Zarathustra: But all that suffers is bent upon life, that it may become ripe and fulsome and full-of-longing. Full of longing for that which is further, higher, clearer.
The Kings and Zarathustra: "I want heirs!"
Zarathustra: Thus speaks all that suffers.
Ugliest Man and Zarathustra: I want children!"
Chorus of Satyrs and Zarathustra: "I don't want me!"
Zarathustra: But pleasure's not set upon heirs, nor children. Pleasure wants itself, wants Eternity, wants Recurrence, wants everything-always the-same-as-it-is. Woe says –
Chorus of Guests and Zarathustra: "Break – bleed, Heart! Roam, Legs! Wings – fly! Onwards! Upwards! Pain!"
Zarathustra: Well now! Come now! O my old Heart –
Chorus of Maenads, Satyrs, and Zarathustra: Woe says –
Chorus of Guests and Zarathustra: "Pass on!"

Bell tolls again.

58 – Exterior. Zarathustra's Cave. Midnight

Zarathustra: You Higher Men, what do you think? Am I a soothsayer? A dreamer? A drunkard? A reader of dreams? A midnight bell? A drop of dew? A mist and air of eternity? Don't you hear it? Can't you smell it? My world is just become perfect. Midnight is midday too. Pain is pleasure. The curse – a blessing. The night is also a sun. Walk away,

or you shall learn – a sage is also a fool! Did you ever say Yes to a single pleasure? O my friends, then thus you said Yes, too – to every woe. All things are enchained, entwined, in love. If ever once you wanted one time twice – if ever once you said –
Chorus of Maenads, Satyrs, and Zarathustra: "You please me, O Happiness! O Happenstance! O Moment's Dance!
Zarathustra: Thus you wanted all of everything to come on back!
Chorus of Maenads, Satyrs, and Zarathustra: All like new, all eternal, all enchained, all entwined, all in love.
Zarathustra: Oh, you so loved the world. You Eternal Ones, love them eternally and forever! And to sorrow, too, you say –
Chorus of Guests and Zarathustra: "Pass on –
Chorus of Maenads, Satyrs, and Zarathustra: – but come on back!" – For all pleasure wants –
Zarathustra: Eternity!

Bell tolls again.

59 – Exterior. Zarathustra's Cave. Midnight

Zarathustra: All pleasure wants the eternity of all things, wants honey, wants zest, wants drunken midnight – wants graves, wants the consolation of graveside tears, wants golden sunsets. What does pleasure not want! She is thirstier, lustier, hungrier, spookier, uncannier than all sorrow. She wants herself. She bites at herself. The Will of the Ring turns in her. She wants love. She wants hate. She is lavish, gives, throws away – begs that someone take her, thanks the taker. Gladly would she be hated. So rich is Pleasure that she lusts after sorrow – after Hell, after Hate, after Shame, after the cripple, after World – after this world. Oh you know her well! You Higher Men, she pines for you. The pleasure, the unbounded, blesséd – for your sorrow, you misfits! All eternal pleasure pines for the misfit, for all eternal pleasure is set upon itself, hence it will have misery too! O Happiness! O Pain! Oh break, Heart! You Higher Men, learn this much at least: Pleasure wants Eternity. Pleasure wants the eternity of all things, wants deep, deep Eternity! Have you now learned my song? Have you divined what it wants? Well now! Come now! You

Higher Men, sing for me now my roundelay. Sing for me now that song whose name is –
Chorus of Maenads, Satyrs, and Zarathustra: "Once Again!"
Zarathustra: Whose meaning is –
Chorus of Maenads, Satyrs, and Zarathustra: "for all Eternity!"
Zarathustra: Sing, you Higher Men! Sing Zarathustra's Roundelay!

The twelfth bell tolls.

Zarathustra: O Mankind attend!
What says the deepest Midnight deep?
Satyrs: "I sleep. I sleep."
Maenads: Wakened from the deepest dream.
Guests: The world is deep –
Zarathustra: – and deeper than the day divined!
Guests: Deep is her woe –
Maenads: Pleasure –
Satyrs: – deeper still than misery.
Zarathustra: Woe says –
Guests and Zarathustra: "Pass on!"
Zarathustra: Yet all pleasure wants –
Satyrs andMaenads: Eternity!
Guests: – wants deep, deep Eternity!

The song is repeated over and over, with the guests gradually taking over more of the parts, until the whole song and dance resembles something of a wild dervish – the guests quite skilfully dancing with the chorus, totally enraptured.

60 – Exterior. Zarathustra's Cave. Early Morning

Zarathustra is sitting on the stone before his cave, as at the beginning. He raises his palms to the morning sun.

Zarathustra: Thou, O Mighty Star – thou deep eye of happenstance – What would all thy happiness be, if thou hadst not those for whom thou shinest? And though they sit encloistered while already thou art awake, and come, and give, and share – how thy proud blush could

The Sign

come to rage for all of that! Well now! They sleep still, these Higher Men, while I am awake. Their ilk is not my kind! It's not for them that I wait here in the mountaintops. I will – to work! to my work, to my day. But they don't understand what the signs of my morning are. My footstep – is for them no wake-up call. Still, they sleep in my cave. Their dream still drinks on my songs of intoxication. But the ear that listens to me – the heedful ear – in them it is – not.

Zarathustra's Eagle dances "overhead."

Zarathustra (*to the eagle*): Well then! That suits – and sits well with me! My animals are awake, for I am awake. My eagle is awake, and honours me like the sun. With eagle's claws he clutches after new light. You are my proper creatures. I love you. But still I lack my proper men!

A sudden flock of doves engulfs Zarathustra.

Zarathustra: What's happening to me?

Zarathustra slowly reclines onto the large stone, playfully fending-off the swarming doves. Groping blindly, his hand becomes entangled in the mane of a lion.

Zarathustra (*sitting up*): The sign is here!

The lion plays at a dance of affection and obedience to Zarathustra, then settles down with him in enjoyment of the now less zealous, but still insistent doves.

Zarathustra: My children are near, my children –

Zarathustra reclines, eyes closed, still. Maenads and a satyr – representing the doves and lion – dance in passive attendance.

61 – Exterior. Zarathustra's Cave. Early Morning

The guests emerge from the cave, and form a train, as if to formally approach Zarathustra. The lion hears them coming, and leaps at them threateningly, with a mighty roar. The guests give out a cry of distress, as with one voice, and vanish quickly back into the cave. Zarathustra sits up, stands, looks around in wonder.

Zarathustra: What's that I hear? Just what has happened to me? Ah! Yes – this is the stone on which I sat but yesterday morning, and hither came the Old Prophet unto me, and here first I heard the cry that just now I heard – The Great Cry Of Distress. O you Higher Men – of *your* distress it was – yes – that the Old Prophet prophesized – to *your* distress it was that he tried to seduce and induce me. "O Zarathustra," he said unto me, "I come to tempt you on to your ultimate sin." To my ultimate sin? (*sits. ponders. leaps up*) Pity! Pity for the Higher Man! Well then! That – had its hearing! My passion and my pity – what lies in all that! Am I striving for happiness? I strive in my work! Well then! The lion is come. My children are near. Zarathustra is ripe and ready. This is my moment. This is my morning. My day is dawning. Hither now, hither, thou great noontide!

END

The *Last Temptation* is, of course, "an interpretation" of Nietzsche's *Also Sprach Zarathustra*, Part Four. The following is the original German. I give no commentary, nor comments, here, except to say that this is **the** *non plus ultra*... If you have no German, then you should get it, even if only for the sake of reading this piece. (And – as is well-known – I recommend, also, that if you have no *Greek*, then you should think about making the attempt to get that too! – if not simply to appreciate Aristophanes' *Birds*, then merely to appreciate the heights to which Nietzsche soars, here, in comparison to, say, Plato... The contrasts between this piece and Plato's *Phaedo*, for instance, are more than merely "instructive")...

Also Sprach Zarathustra

Vierter und letzter Theil

∞

FRIEDRICH NIETZSCHE

Ach, wo in der Welt
geschahen grössere Thorheiten,
als bei den Mitleidigen?
Und was in der Welt stiftete mehr Leid,
als die Thorheiten der Mitleidigen?
Wehe allen Liebenden,
die nicht noch eine Höhe haben,
welche über ihrem Mitleiden ist!
Also sprach der Teufel einst zu mir:
"auch Gott hat seine Hölle:
das ist seine Liebe zu den Menschen."
Und jüngst hörte ich ihn dies Wort sagen:
"Gott ist todt;
an seinem Mitleiden mit den Menschen
ist Gott gestorben."

Also Sprach Zarathustra, Zweiter Theil:
- Von den Mitleidigen

Das Honig=Opfer

Und wieder liefen Monde und Jahre über Zarathustras Seele, und er achtete dessen nicht; sein Haar aber wurde weiss. Eines Tages, als er auf einem Steine vor seiner Höhle sass und still hinausschaute, – man schaut aber dort auf das Meer hinaus, und hinweg über gewundene Abgründe – da giengen seine Thiere nachdenklich um ihn herum und stellten sich endlich vor ihn hin.
"O Zarathustra, sagten sie, schaust du wohl aus nach deinem Glücke?" – "Was liegt am Glücke! antwortete er, ich trachte lange nicht mehr nach Glücke, ich trachte nach meinem Werke." – "O Zarathustra, redeten die Thiere abermals, Das sagst du als Einer, der des Guten übergenug hat. Liegst du nicht in einem himmelblauen See von Glück?" – "Ihr Schalks=Narren, antwortete Zarathustra und lächelte, wie gut wähltet ihr das Gleichniss! Aber ihr wißt auch, daß mein Glück schwer ist und nicht wie eine flüssige Wasserwelle: es drängt mich und will nicht von mir und thut gleich geschmolzenem Peche." –

Da giengen die Thiere wieder nachdenklich um ihn herum und stellten sich dann abermals vor ihn hin. "O Zarathustra, sagten sie, daher also kommt es, daß du selber immer gelber und dunkler wirst, obschon dein Haar weiss und flächsern aussehen will? Siehe doch, du sitzest in deinem Peche!" – "Was sagt ihr da, meine Thiere, sagte Zarathustra und lachte dazu, wahrlich, ich lästerte als ich von Peche sprach. Wie mir geschieht, so geht es allen Früchten, die reif werden. Es ist der Honig in meinen Adern, der mein Blut dicker und auch meine Seele stiller macht." – "So wird es sein, O Zarathustra, antworteten die Thiere und drängten sich an ihn; willst du aber nicht heute auf einen hohen Berg steigen? Die Luft ist rein, und man sieht heute mehr von der Welt als jemals." – "Ja, meine Thiere, antwortete er, ihr rathet trefflich und mir nach dem Herzen: ich will heute auf einen hohen Berg steigen! Aber sorgt, daß dort Honig mir zur Hand sei, gelber, weisser, guter, eisfrischer Waben=Goldhonig. Denn wisset, ich will droben das Honig=Opfer bringen." –

Als Zarathustra aber oben auf der Höhe war, sandte er die Thiere heim, die ihn geleitet hatten, und fand, daß er nunmehr allein sei: – da lachte er aus ganzem Herzen, sah sich um und sprach also:

Daß ich von Opfern sprach und Honig-Opfern, eine List war's nur meiner Rede und, wahrlich, eine nützliche Thorheit! Hier oben darf ich schon freier reden, als vor Einsiedler-Höhlen und Einsiedler-Hausthieren.

Was opfern! Ich verschwende, was mir geschenkt wird, ich Verschwender mit tausend Händen: wie dürfte ich Das noch – Opfern heissen!

Und als ich nach Honig begehrte, begehrte ich nur nach Köder und süssem Seime und Schleime, nach dem auch Brummbären und wunderliche mürrische böse Vögel die Zunge lecken:

– nach dem besten Köder, wie er Jägern und Fischfängern noththut. Denn wenn die Welt wie ein dunkler Thierwald ist und aller wilden Jäger Lustgarten, so dünkt sie mich noch mehr und lieber ein abgründliches reiches Meer,

– ein Meer voll bunter Fische und Krebse, nach dem es auch Götter gelüsten möchte, daß sie an ihm zu Fischern würden und zu Netz-Auswerfern: so reich ist die Welt an Wunderlichem, grossem und kleinem!

Sonderlich die Menschen-Welt, das Menschen-Meer: – nach dem werfe ich nun meine goldene Angelruthe aus und spreche: thue dich auf, du Menschen-Abgrund!

Thue dich auf und wirf mir deine Fische und Glitzer-Krebse zu! Mit meinem besten Köder ködere ich mir heute die wunderlichsten Menschen-Fische!

– mein Glück selber werfe ich hinaus in alle Weiten und Fernen, zwischen Aufgang, Mittag und Niedergang, ob nicht an meinem Glücke viele Menschen-Fische zerrn und zappeln lernen.

bis sie, anbeissend an meine spitzen verborgenen Haken, hinauf müssen in meine Höhe, die buntesten Abgrund-Gründlinge zu dem boshaftigsten aller Menschen-Fischfänger.

Der nämlich bin ich von Grund und Anbeginn, ziehend, heranziehend, hinaufziehend, aufziehend, ein Zieher, Züchter und Zuchtmeister, der sich nicht umsonst einstmals zusprach: "Werde, der du bist!"

Also mögen nunmehr die Menschen zu mir hinauf kommen: denn noch warte ich der Zeichen, daß es Zeit sei zu meinem Niedergange, noch gehe ich selber nicht unter, wie ich muss, unter Menschen.

Das Honig-Opfer

Dazu warte ich hier, listig und spöttisch auf hohen Bergen, kein Ungeduldiger, kein Geduldiger, vielmehr Einer, der auch die Geduld verlernt hat, – weil er nicht mehr "duldet."

Mein Schicksal nämlich läßt mir Zeit: es vergass mich wohl? Oder sitzt es hinter einem grossen Steine im Schatten und fängt Fliegen?

Und wahrlich, ich bin ihm gut darob, meinem ewigen Schicksale, dass es mich nicht hetzt und drängt und mir Zeit zu Possen läßt und Bosheiten: also daß ich heute zu einem Fischfange auf diesen hohen Berg stieg.

Fieng wohl je ein Mensch auf hohen Bergen Fische? Und wenn es auch eine Thorheit ist, was ich hier oben will und treibe: besser noch Dies, als daß ich da unten feierlich würde vor Warten und grün und gelb –

– ein gespreizter Zornschnauber vor Warten, ein heiliger Heule-Sturm aus Bergen, ein Ungeduldiger, der in die Thäler hinabruft: "Hört, oder ich peitsche euch mit der Geissel Gottes!"

Nicht daß ich solchen Zürnern darob gram würde: zum Lachen sind sie mir gut genung! Ungeduldig müssen sie schon sein, diese grossen Lärmtrommeln, welche heute oder niemals zu Worte kommen!

Ich aber und mein Schicksal – wir reden nicht zum Heute, wir reden auch nicht zum Niemals: wir haben zum Reden schon Geduld und Zeit und Überzeit. Denn einst muss er doch kommen und darf nicht vorübergehn.

Wer muss einst kommen und darf nicht vorübergehn? Unser grosser Hazar, das ist unser grosses fernes Menschen-Reich, das Zarathustra-Reich von tausend Jahren – –

Wie ferne mag solches "Ferne" sein? was geht's mich an! Aber darum steht es mir doch nicht minder fest –, mit beiden Füssen stehe ich sicher auf diesem Grunde,

– auf einem ewigen Grunde, auf hartem Urgesteine, auf diesem höchsten härtesten Urgebirge, zu dem alle Winde kommen als zur Wetterscheide, fragend nach Wo? und Woher? und Wohinaus?

Hier lache, lache meine helle heile Bosheit! Von hohen Bergen wirf hinab dein glitzerndes Spott-Gelächter! Ködere mit deinem Glitzern mir die schönsten Menschen-Fische!

Und was in allen Meeren mir zugehört, mein An-und-für-mich in allen Dingen — Das fische mir heraus, Das führe zu mir herauf: dess warte ich, der boshaftigste aller Fischfänger.

Hinaus, hinaus, meine Angel! Hinein, hinab, Köder meines Glücks! Träufle deinen süssesten Thau, mein Herzens-Honig! Beisse, meine Angel, in den Bauch aller schwarzen Trübsal!

Hinaus, hinaus, mein Auge! Oh welche vielen Meere rings um mich, welch dämmernde Menschen-Zukünfte! Und über mir — welch rosenrothe Stille! Welch entwölktes Schweigen!

Der Nothschrei

Des nächsten Tages sass Zarathustra wieder auf seinem Steine vor der Höhle, während die Thiere draussen in der Welt herumschweiften, dass sie neue Nahrung heimbrächten, – auch neuen Honig: denn Zarathustra hatte den alten Honig bis auf das letzte Korn verthan und verschwendet. Als er aber dermaassen dasass, mit einem Stecken in der Hand, und den Schatten seiner Gestalt auf der Erde abzeichnete, nachdenkend und, wahrlich! nicht über sich und seinen Schatten – da erschrak er mit Einem Male und fuhr zusammen: denn er sahe neben seinem Schatten noch einen andern Schatten. Und wie er schnell um sich blickte und aufstand, siehe, da stand der Wahrsager neben ihm, der selbe, den er einstmals an seinem Tische gespeist und getränkt hatte, der Verkündiger der grossen Müdigkeit, welcher lehrte: "Alles ist gleich, es lohnt sich Nichts, Welt ist ohne Sinn, Wissen würgt." Aber sein Antlitz hatte sich inzwischen verwandelt; und als ihm Zarathustra in die Augen blickte, wurde sein Herz abermals erschreckt: so viel schlimme Verkündigungen und aschgraue Blitze liefen über dies Gesicht.

Der Wahrsager, der es wahrgenommen, was sich in Zarathustras Seele zutrug, wischte mit der Hand über sein Antlitz hin, wie als ob er dasselbe wegwischen wollte; desgleichen that auch Zarathustra. Und als Beide dergestalt sich schweigend gefaßt und gekräftigt hatten, gaben sie sich die Hände, zum Zeichen, daß sie sich wiedererkennen wollten.

"Sei mir willkommen, sagte Zarathustra, du Wahrsager der grossen Müdigkeit, du sollst nicht umsonst einstmals mein Tisch- und Gastfreund gewesen sein. Iss und trink auch heute bei mir und vergieb es, daß ein vergnügter alter Mann mit dir zu Tische sitzt!" – "Ein vergnügter alter Mann? antwortete der Wahrsager, den Kopf schüttelnd: wer du aber auch bist oder sein willst, O Zarathustra, du bist es zum Längsten hier Oben gewesen, – dein Nachen soll über Kurzem nicht mehr im Trocknen sitzen!" – "Sitze ich denn im Trocknen?" fragte Zarathustra lachend. – "Die Wellen um deinen Berg, antwortete der Wahrsager, steigen und steigen, die Wellen grosser Noth und Trübsal: die werden bald auch deinen Nachen heben und dich davontragen." – Zarathustra schwieg hierauf und wunderte sich. – "Hörst du noch Nichts? fuhr der Wahrsager fort: rauscht und braust es nicht herauf aus der Tiefe?" – Zarathustra schwieg abermals und horchte: da hörte er einen langen,

langen Schrei, welchen die Abgründe sich zuwarfen und weitergaben, denn keiner wollte ihn behalten: so böse klang er.

"Du schlimmer Verkündiger, sprach endlich Zarathustra, das ist ein Nothschrei und der Schrei eines Menschen, der mag wohl aus einem schwarzen Meere kommen. Aber was geht mich Menschen-Noth an! Meine letzte Sünde, die mir aufgespart blieb, – weißt du wohl, wie sie heißt?"

– "Mitleiden! antwortete der Wahrsager aus einem überströmenden Herzen und hob beide Hände empor – O Zarathustra, ich komme, daß ich dich zu deiner letzten Sünde verführe!"

– Und kaum waren diese Worte gesprochen, da erscholl der Schrei abermals, und länger und ängstlicher als vorher, auch schon viel näher. "Hörst du? Hörst du, O Zarathustra? rief der Wahrsager, dir gilt der Schrei, dich ruft er: komm, komm, komm, es ist Zeit, es ist höchste Zeit!" –

Zarathustra schwieg hierauf, verwirrt und erschüttert; endlich fragte er, wie Einer, der bei sich selber zögert: "Und wer ist das, der dort mich ruft?"

"Aber du weißt es ja, antwortete der Wahrsager heftig, was verbirgst du dich? Der höhere Mensch ist es, der nach dir schreit!"

"Der höhere Mensch? schrie Zarathustra von Grausen erfaßt: was will der? Was will der? Der höhere Mensch! Was will der hier?" – und seine Haut bedeckte sich mit Schweiss.

Der Wahrsager aber antwortete nicht auf die Angst Zarathustras, sondern horchte und horchte nach der Tiefe zu. Als es jedoch lange Zeit dort stille blieb, wandte er seinen Blick zurück und sahe Zarathustra stehn und zittern.

"O Zarathustra, hob er mit trauriger Stimme an, du stehst nicht da wie Einer, den sein Glück drehend macht: du wirst tanzen müssen, daß du mir nicht umfällst!

Aber wenn du auch vor mir tanzen wolltest und alle deine Saitensprünge springen: Niemand soll mir doch sagen dürfen: ‚Siehe, hier tanzt der letzte frohe Mensch!'

Umsonst käme Einer auf diese Höhe, der den hier suchte: Höhlen fände er wohl und Hinter-Höhlen, Verstecke für Verstackte, aber nicht Glücks-Schachte und Schatzkammern und neue Glücks-Goldadern.

Glück – wie fände man wohl das Glück bei solchen Vergrabenen und Einsiedlern! Muss ich das letzte Glück noch auf glückseligen Inseln suchen und ferne zwischen vergessenen Meeren?

Aber Alles ist gleich, es lohnt sich Nichts, es hilft kein Suchen, es giebt auch keine glückseligen Inseln mehr!" –

– Also seufzte der Wahrsager; bei seinem letzten Seufzer aber wurde Zarathustra wieder hell und sicher, gleich Einem, der aus einem tiefen Schlunde an's Licht kommt. "Nein! Nein! Dreimal Nein! rief er mit starker Stimme und strich sich den Bart – Das weiss ich besser! Es giebt noch glückselige Inseln! Stille davon, du seufzender Trauersack!

Höre davon auf zu plätschern, du Regenwolke am Vormittag! Stehe ich denn nicht schon da, nass von deiner Trübsal und begossen wie ein Hund?

Nun schüttle ich mich und laufe dir davon, dass ich wieder trocken werde: dess darfst du nicht Wunder haben! Dünke ich dir unhöflich? Aber hier ist mein Hof.

Was aber deinen höheren Menschen angeht: wohlan! ich suche ihn flugs in jenen Wäldern: daher kam sein Schrei. Vielleicht bedrängt ihn da ein böses Thier.

Er ist in meinem Bereiche: darin soll er mir nicht zu Schaden kommen! Und wahrlich, es giebt viele böse Thiere bei mir."

– Mit diesen Worten wandte sich Zarathustra zum Gehen. Da sprach der Wahrsager: "O Zarathustra, du bist ein Schelm!

Ich weiss es schon: du willst mich los sein! Lieber noch läufst du in die Wälder und stellst bösen Thieren nach!

Aber was hilft es dir? Des Abends wirst du doch mich wiederhaben, in deiner eignen Höhle werde ich dasitzen, geduldig und schwer wie ein Klotz – und auf dich warten!"

"So sei's! rief Zarathustra zurück im Fortgehn: und was mein ist in meiner Höhle, gehört auch dir, meinem Gastfreunde!

Solltest du aber drin noch Honig finden, wohlan! so lecke ihn nur auf, du Brummbär, und versüsse deine Seele! Am Abende nämlich wollen wir Beide guter Dinge sein,

– guter Dinge und froh darob, dass dieser Tag zu Ende gieng! Und du selber sollst zu meinen Liedern als mein Tanzbär tanzen.

Du glaubst nicht daran? Du schüttelst den Kopf? Wohlan! Wohlauf! Alter Bär! Aber auch ich – bin ein Wahrsager."

Also sprach Zarathustra.

Gespräch mit den Königen

1.

Zarathustra war noch keine Stunde in seinen Bergen und Wäldern unterwegs, da sahe er mit Einem Male einen seltsamen Aufzug. Gerade auf dem Wege, den er hinabwollte, kamen zwei Könige gegangen, mit Kronen und Purpurgürteln geschmückt und bunt wie flamingo=Vögel: die trieben einen beladenen Esel vor sich her. "Was wollen diese Könige in meinem Reiche?" sprach Zarathustra erstaunt zu seinem Herzen und versteckte sich geschwind hinter einem Busche. Als aber die Könige bis zu ihm herankamen, sagte er, halblaut, wie Einer, der zu sich allein redet: "Seltsam! Seltsam! Wie reimt sich Das zusammen? Zwei Könige sehe ich – und nur Einen Esel!" Da machten die beiden Könige Halt, lächelten, sahen nach der Stelle hin, woher die Stimme kam, und sahen sich nachher selber in's Gesicht. "Solcherlei denkt man wohl auch unter uns, sagte der König zur Rechten, aber man spricht es nicht aus."

Der König zur Linken aber zuckte mit den Achseln und antwortete: "Das mag wohl ein Ziegenhirt sein. Oder ein Einsiedler, der zu lange unter Felsen und Bäumen lebte. Gar keine Gesellschaft nämlich verdirbt auch die guten Sitten."

"Die guten Sitten! entgegnete unwillig und bitter der andre König: wem laufen wir denn aus dem Wege? ist es nicht den 'guten Sitten'? Unsrer 'guten Gesellschaft'?

Lieber, wahrlich, unter Einsiedlern und Ziegenhirten als mit unserm vergoldeten falschen überschminkten Pöbel leben, – ob er sich schon 'gute Gesellschaft' heißt,

– ob er sich schon 'Adel' heißt. Aber da ist Alles falsch und faul, voran das Blut, Dank alten schlechten Krankheiten und schlechteren Heil=Künstlern.

Der Beste und Liebste ist mir heute noch ein gesunder Bauer, grob, listig, hartnäckig, langhaltig: das ist heute die vornehmste Art.

Der Bauer ist heute der Beste; und Bauern=Art sollte Herr sein! Aber es ist das Reich des Pöbels, – ich lasse mir Nichts mehr vormachen. Pöbel aber, das heißt: Mischmasch.

Pöbel=Mischmasch: darin ist Alles in Allem durcheinander, Heiliger und Hallunke und Junker und Jude und jegliches Vieh aus der Arche Noäh.

Gespräch mit den Königen

Gute Sitten! Alles ist bei uns falsch und faul. Niemand weiss mehr zu verehren: dem gerade laufen wir davon. Es sind süssliche zudringliche Hunde, sie vergolden Palmenblätter.

Dieser Ekel würgt mich, daß wir Könige selber falsch wurden, überhängt und verkleidet durch alten vergilbten Grossväter-Prunk, Schaumünzen für die Dümmsten und die Schlauesten, und wer heute Alles mit der Macht Schacher treibt!

Wir sind nicht die Ersten – und müssen es doch bedeuten: dieser Betrügerei sind wir endlich satt und ekel geworden.

Dem Gesindel giengen wir aus dem Wege, allen diesen Schreihälsen und Schreib-Schmeissfliegen, dem Krämer-Gestank, dem Ehrgeiz-Gezappel, dem üblen Athem –: pfui, unter dem Gesindel leben,

– pfui, unter dem Gesindel die Ersten zu bedeuten! Ach, Ekel! Ekel! Ekel! Was liegt noch an uns Königen!" –

"Deine alte Krankheit fällt dich an, sagte hier der König zur Linken, der Ekel fällt dich an, mein armer Bruder. Aber du weißt es doch, es hört uns Einer zu."

Sofort erhob sich Zarathustra, der zu diesen Reden Ohren und Augen aufgesperrt hatte, aus seinem Schlupfwinkel, trat auf die Könige zu und begann:

"Der Euch zuhört, der Euch gerne zuhört, ihr Könige, der heißt Zarathustra.

Ich bin Zarathustra, der einst sprach: 'Was liegt noch an Königen!' Vergebt mir, ich freute mich, als Ihr zu einander sagtet: 'Was liegt an uns Königen!'

Hier aber ist mein Reich und meine Herrschaft: was mögt Ihr wohl in meinem Reiche suchen? Vielleicht aber fandet Ihr unterwegs, was ich suche: nämlich den höheren Menschen."

Als Dies die Könige hörten, schlugen sie sich an die Brust und sprachen mit Einem Munde: "Wir sind erkannt!

Mit dem Schwerte dieses Wortes zerhaust du unsres Herzens dickste Finsterniss. Du entdecktest unsre Noth, denn siehe! Wir sind unterwegs, daß wir den höheren Menschen fänden –

– den Menschen, der höher ist als wir: ob wir gleich Könige sind. Ihm führen wir diesen Esel zu. Der höchste Mensch nämlich soll auf Erden auch der höchste Herr sein.

Es giebt kein härteres Unglück in allem Menschen-Schicksale, als wenn die Mächtigen der Erde nicht auch die ersten Menschen sind. Da wird Alles falsch und schief und ungeheuer.

Und wann sie gar die letzten sind und mehr Vieh als Mensch: da steigt und steigt der Pöbel im Preise, und endlich spricht gar die Pöbel-Tugend: 'siehe, ich allein bin Tugend!' –
Was hörte ich eben? antwortete Zarathustra; welche Weisheit bei Königen! Ich bin entzückt, und, wahrlich, schon gelüstet's mich, einen Reim darauf zu machen: –
– mag es auch ein Reim werden, der nicht für Jedermanns Ohren taugt. Ich verlernte seit langem schon die Rücksicht auf lange Ohren. Wohlan! Wohlauf!
(Hier aber geschah es, daß auch der Esel zu Worte kam: er sagte aber deutlich und mit bösem Willen I-A.)

"Einstmals – ich glaub', im Jahr des Heiles Eins –
Sprach die Sibylle, trunken sonder Weins:
'Weh, nun geht's schief!
Verfall! Verfall! Nie sank die Welt so tief!
Rom sank zur Hure und zur Huren-Bude,
Roms Caesar sank zum Vieh, Gott selbst – ward Jude!'"

2.

An diesen Reimen Zarathustras weideten sich die Könige; der König zur Rechten aber sprach: "O Zarathustra, wie gut thaten wir, daß wir auszogen, dich zu sehn!
Deine Feinde nämlich zeigten uns dein Bild in ihrem Spiegel: da blicktest du mit der Fratze eines Teufels und hohnlachend: also daß wir uns vor dir fürchteten.
Aber was half's! Immer wieder stachst du uns in Ohr und Herz mit deinen Sprüchen. Da sprachen wir endlich: was liegt daran, wie er aussieht!
Wir müssen ihn hören, ihn, der lehrt 'ihr sollt den Frieden lieben als Mittel zu neuen Kriegen, und den kurzen Frieden mehr als den langen!'
Niemand sprach je so kriegerische Worte: 'Was ist gut? Tapfer sein ist gut. Der gute Krieg ist's, der jede Sache heiligt.'
O Zarathustra, unsrer Väter Blut rührte sich bei solchen Worten in unserm Leibe: das war wie die Rede des Frühlings zu alten Weinfässern.
Wenn die Schwerter durcheinander liefen gleich rothgefleckten Schlangen, da wurden unsre Väter dem Leben gut; alles Friedens Sonne dünkte sie flau und lau, der lange Frieden aber machte Scham.

Gespräch mit den Königen

Wie sie seufzten, unsre Väter, wenn sie an der Wand blitzblanke ausgedorrte Schwerter sahen! Denen gleich dürsteten sie nach Krieg. Ein Schwert nämlich will Blut trinken und funkelt vor Begierde." --
- Als die Könige dergestalt mit Eifer von dem Glück ihrer Väter redeten und schwätzten, überkam Zarathustra keine kleine Lust, ihres Eifers zu spotten: denn ersichtlich waren es sehr friedfertige Könige, welche er vor sich sah, solche mit alten und feinen Gesichtern. Aber er bezwang sich. "Wohlan! sprach er, dorthin führt der Weg, da liegt die Höhle Zarathustras; und dieser Tag soll einen langen Abend haben! Jetzt aber ruft mich eilig ein Nothschrei fort von Euch.

Es ehrt meine Höhle, wenn Könige in ihr sitzen und warten wollen: aber, freilich, Ihr werdet lange warten müssen!

Je nun! Was thut's! Wo lernt man heute besser warten als an Höfen? Und der Könige ganze Tugend, die ihnen übrig blieb, - heißt sie heute nicht: Warten-können?"

Also sprach Zarathustra.

Der Blutegel

Und Zarathustra gieng nachdenklich weiter und tiefer, durch Wälder und vorbei an moorigen Gründen; wie es aber Jedem ergeht, der über schwere Dinge nachdenkt, so trat er unversehens dabei auf einen Menschen. Und siehe, da sprützten ihm mit Einem Male ein Wehschrei und zwei Flüche und zwanzig schlimme Schimpfworte in's Gesicht: also daß er in seinem Schrecken den Stock erhob und auch auf den Getretenen noch zuschlug. Gleich darauf aber kam ihm die Besinnung; und sein Herz lachte über die Thorheit, die er eben gethan hatte.

"Vergieb, sagte er zu dem Getretenen, der sich grimmig erhoben und gesetzt hatte, vergieb und vernimm vor Allem erst ein Gleichniss.

Wie ein Wanderer, der von fernen Dingen träumt, unversehens auf einsamer Strasse einen schlafenden Hund anstösst, einen Hund, der in der Sonne liegt:

– wie da Beide auffahren, sich anfahren, Todfeinden gleich, diese zwei zu Tod Erschrockenen: also ergieng es uns.

Und doch! Und doch – wie wenig hat gefehlt, daß sie einander liebkosten, dieser Hund und dieser Einsame! Sind sie doch Beide – Einsame!"

– "Wer du auch sein magst, sagte immer noch grimmig der Getretene, du trittst mir auch mit deinem Gleichniss zu nahe, und nicht nur mit deinem Fusse!

Siehe doch, bin ich denn ein Hund?" – und dabei erhob sich der Sitzende und zog seinen nackten Arm aus dem Sumpfe. Zuerst nämlich hatte er ausgestreckt am Boden gelegen, verborgen und unkenntlich gleich Solchen, die einem Sumpf-Wilde auflauern.

"Aber was treibst du doch!" rief Zarathustra erschreckt, denn er sahe, daß über den nackten Arm weg viel Blut floss, – was ist dir zugestossen? Biss dich, du Unseliger, ein schlimmes Thier?

Der Blutende lachte, immer noch erzürnt. "Was geht's dich an! sagte er und wollte weitergehn. Hier bin ich heim und in meinem Bereiche. Mag mich fragen, wer da will: einem Tölpel aber werde ich schwerlich antworten."

"Du irrst, sagte Zarathustra mitleidig und hielt ihn fest, du irrst: hier bist du nicht bei dir, sondern in meinem Reiche, und darin soll mir Keiner zu Schaden kommen.

Nenne mich aber immerhin, wie du willst, – ich bin, der ich sein muss. Ich selber heisse mich Zarathustra.

Wohlan! Dort hinauf geht der Weg zu Zarathustras Höhle: die ist nicht fern, – willst du nicht bei mir deiner Wunden warten?

Es gieng dir schlimm, du Unseliger, in diesem Leben: erst biss dich das Thier, und dann – trat dich der Mensch!" –

– Als aber der Getretene den Namen Zarathustras hörte, verwandelte er sich. "Was geschieht mir doch! rief er aus, wer kümmert mich denn noch in diesem Leben, als dieser Eine Mensch, nämlich Zarathustra, und jenes Eine Thier, das vom Blute lebt, der Blutegel?

Des Blutegels halber lag ich hier an diesem Sumpfe wie ein Fischer, und schon war mein ausgehängter Arm zehn Mal angebissen, da beisst noch ein schönerer Igel nach meinem Blute, Zarathustra selber!

Oh Glück! Oh Wunder! Gelobt sei dieser Tag, der mich in diesen Sumpf lockte! Gelobt sei der beste lebendigste Schröpfkopf, der heut lebt, gelobt sei der grosse Gewissens=Blutegel Zarathustra!" –

Also sprach der Getretene; und Zarathustra freute sich über seine Worte und ihre feine ehrfürchtige Art. "Wer bist du? fragte er und reichte ihm die Hand, zwischen uns bleibt Viel aufzuklären und aufzuheitern: aber schon, dünkt mich, wird es reiner heller Tag."

"Ich bin *der Gewissenhafte des Geistes*, antwortete der Gefragte, und in Dingen des Geistes nimmt es nicht leicht Einer strenger, enger und härter als ich, ausgenommen der, von dem ich's lernte, Zarathustra selber.

Lieber Nichts wissen, als Vieles halb wissen! Lieber ein Narr sein auf eigne Faust, als ein Weiser nach fremdem Gutdünken! Ich – gehe auf den Grund:

– was liegt daran, ob er gross oder klein ist? Ob er Sumpf oder Himmel heisst? Eine Hand breit Grund ist mir genung: wenn er nur wirklich Grund und Boden ist!

– eine Hand breit Grund: darauf kann man stehn. In der rechten Wissen=Gewissenschaft giebt es nichts Grosses und nichts Kleines."

"So bist du vielleicht der Erkenner des Blutegels? fragte Zarathustra; und du gehst dem Blutegel nach bis auf die letzten Gründe, du Gewissenhafter?"

"O Zarathustra, antwortete der Getretene, das wäre ein Ungeheures, wie dürfte ich mich dessen unterfangen!

Wess ich aber Meister und Kenner bin, das ist des Blutegels Hirn: – das ist *meine* Welt!

Und es ist auch eine Welt! Vergieb aber, daß hier mein Stolz zu Worte kommt, denn ich habe hier nicht meines Gleichen. Darum sprach ich ‚hier bin ich heim.'

Wie lange gehe ich schon diesem Einen nach, dem Hirn des Blutegels, daß die schlüpfrige Wahrheit mir hier nicht mehr entschlüpfe! Hier ist mein Reich!

– darob warf ich alles Andere fort, darob wurde mir alles Andre gleich; und dicht neben meinem Wissen lagert mein schwarzes Unwissen.

Mein Gewissen des Geistes will es so von mir, daß ich Eins weiss und sonst Alles nicht weiss: es ekelt mich aller Halben des Geistes, aller Dunstigen, Schwebenden, Schwärmerischen.

Wo meine Redlichkeit aufhört, bin ich blind und will auch blind sein. Wo ich aber wissen will, will ich auch redlich sein, nämlich hart, streng, eng, grausam, unerbittlich.

Daß du einst sprachst, O Zarathustra: ‚Geist ist das Leben, das selber in's Leben schneidet,' das führte und verführte mich zu deiner Lehre. Und, wahrlich, mit eignem Blute mehrte ich mir das eigne Wissen!"

– "Wie der Augenschein lehrt," fiel Zarathustra ein; denn immer noch floss das Blut an dem nackten Arme des Gewissenhaften herab. Es hatten nämlich zehn Blutegel sich in denselben eingebissen.

"Oh du wunderlicher Gesell, wie Viel lehrt mich dieser Augenschein da, nämlich du selber! Und nicht Alles dürfte ich vielleicht in deine strengen Ohren giessen!

Wohlan! So scheiden wir hier! Doch möchte ich gerne dich wiederfinden. Dort hinauf führt der Weg zu meiner Höhle: heute Nacht sollst du dort mein lieber Gast sein!

Gerne möchte ich's auch an deinem Leibe wieder gut machen, daß Zarathustra dich mit Füssen trat: darüber denke ich nach. Jetzt aber ruft mich ein Nothschrei eilig fort von dir."

Also sprach Zarathustra.

Der Zauberer

1.

Als aber Zarathustra um einen Felsen herumbog, da sahe er, nicht weit unter sich, auf dem gleichen Wege, einen Menschen, der die Glieder warf wie ein Tobsüchtiger und endlich bäuchlings zur Erde niederstürzte. "Halt! sprach da Zarathustra zu seinem Herzen, Der dort muss wohl der höhere Mensch sein, von ihm kam jener schlimme Nothschrei, – ich will sehn, ob da zu helfen ist." Als er aber hinzulief, an die Stelle, wo der Mensch auf dem Boden lag, fand er einen zitternden alten Mann mit stieren Augen; und wie sehr sich Zarathustra mühte, dass er ihn aufrichte und wieder auf seine Beine stelle, es war umsonst. Auch schien der Unglückliche nicht zu merken, dass jemand um ihn sei; vielmehr sah er sich immer mit rührenden Gebärden um, wie ein von aller Welt Verlassener und Vereinsamter. Zuletzt aber, nach vielem Zittern, Zucken und Sich-zusammen-Krümmen, begann er also zu jammern:

> Wer wärmt mich, wer liebt mich noch?
> Gebt heisse Hände!
> Gebt Herzens-Kohlenbecken!
> Hingestreckt, schaudernd,
> Halbtodtem gleich, dem man die Füsse wärmt –
> Geschüttelt, ach! von unbekannten Fiebern,
> Zitternd vor spitzen eisigen Frost-Pfeilen,
> Von dir gejagt, Gedanke!
> Unnennbarer! Verhüllter! Entsetzlicher!
> Du Jäger hinter Wolken!
> Darniedergeblitzt von dir,
> Du höhnisch Auge, das mich aus Dunklem anblickt: – so liege ich,

> Biege mich, winde mich, gequält
> Von allen ewigen Martern,
> Getroffen
> Von Dir, grausamster Jäger,
> Du unbekannter – Gott!

Triff tiefer,
Triff einmal noch!
Zerstich, zerbrich dies Herz!
Was soll dies Martern
Mit zähnestumpfen Pfeilen?
Was blickst du wieder,
Der Menschen-Qual nicht müde,
Mit schadenfrohen Götter-Blitz-Augen?
Nicht tödten willst du,
Nur martern, martern?
Wozu – mich martern,
Du schadenfroher unbekannter Gott? –

Haha! Du schleichst heran?
Bei solcher Mitternacht
Was willst du? Sprich!
Du drängst mich, drückst mich –
Ha! schon viel zu nahe!
Weg! Weg!
Du hörst mich athmen,
Du behorchst mein Herz,
Du Eifersüchtiger –
Worauf doch eifersüchtig?
Weg! Weg! Wozu die Leiter?
Willst du hinein,
In's Herz,
Einsteigen, in meine heimlichsten
Gedanken einsteigen?
Schamloser! Unbekannter – Dieb!
Was willst du dir erstehlen,
Was willst du dir erhorchen,
Was willst du dir erfoltern,
Du Folterer!
Du – Henker-Gott!
Oder soll ich, dem Hunde gleich,
Vor dir mich wälzen?
Hingebend, begeistert-ausser-mir,
Dir – Liebe zuwedeln?

Umsonst! Stich weiter,
Grausamster Stachel! Nein,
Kein Hund – dein Wild nur bin ich,
Grausamster Jäger!
Dein stolzester Gefangner,
Du Räuber hinter Wolken!
Sprich endlich,
Was willst du, Wegelagerer, von mir?
Du Blitz-Verhüllter! Unbekannter! Sprich,

Was willst du, unbekannter Gott? – –
Wie? Lösegeld?
Was willst du Lösegelds?
Verlange Viel – das räth mein Stolz!
Und rede kurz – das räth mein andrer Stolz!

Haha!
Mich – willst du? Mich?
Mich – ganz?

Haha!
Und marterst mich, Narr, der du bist,
Zermarterst meinen Stolz?
Gieb Liebe mir – wer wärmt mich noch?
Wer liebt mich noch? – gieb heisse Hände,
Gieb Herzens-Kohlenbecken,
Gieb mir, dem Einsamsten,
Den Eis, ach! siebenfaches Eis
Nach Feinden selber,
Nach Feinden schmachten lehrt,
Gieb, ja ergieb,
Grausamster Feind,
Mir – dich! – –
Davon!

Da floh er selber,
Mein letzter einziger Genoss,
Mein grosser Feind,
Mein Unbekannter,
Mein Henker-Gott! –

– Nein! Komm zurück,
Mit allen deinen Martern!
Zum Letzten aller Einsamen
Oh komm zurück!
All meine Thränen-Bäche laufen
Zu dir den Lauf!

Und meine letzte Herzens-Flamme –
Dir glüht sie auf!
Oh komm zurück,
Mein unbekannter Gott! Mein Schmerz! Mein letztes – Glück!

2.

– Hier aber konnte sich Zarathustra nicht länger halten, nahm seinen Stock und schlug mit allen Kräften auf den Jammernden los. "Halt ein! schrie er ihm zu, mit ingrimmigem Lachen, halt ein, du Schauspieler! Du Falschmünzer! Du Lügner aus dem Grunde! Ich erkenne dich wohl!

Ich will dir schon warme Beine machen, du schlimmer Zauberer, ich verstehe mich gut darauf, Solchen wie du bist – einzuheizen!"

– "Lass ab, sagte der alte Mann und sprang vom Boden auf, schlage nicht mehr, O Zarathustra! Ich trieb's also nur zum Spiele!

Solcherlei gehört zu meiner Kunst; dich selber wollte ich auf die Probe stellen, als ich dir diese Probe gab! Und, wahrlich, du hast mich gut durchschaut!

Aber auch du – gabst mir von dir keine kleine Probe: du bist hart, du weiser Zarathustra! Hart schlägst du zu mit deinen 'Wahrheiten', dein Knüttel erzwingt von mir – diese Wahrheit!"

– "Schmeichle nicht, antwortete Zarathustra, immer noch erregt und finsterblickend, du Schauspieler aus dem Grunde! Du bist falsch: was redest du – von Wahrheit!

Du Pfau der Pfauen, du Meer der Eitelkeit, was spieltest du vor mir, du schlimmer Zauberer, an wen sollte ich glauben, als du in solcher Gestalt jammertest?"

"Den Büsser des Geistes, sagte der alte Mann, den – spielte ich: du selber erfandest einst dies Wort –

– den Dichter und Zauberer, der gegen sich selber endlich seinen Geist wendet, den Verwandelten, der an seinem bösen Wissen und Gewissen erfriert.

Und gesteh es nur ein: es währte lange, O Zarathustra, bis du hinter meine Kunst und Lüge kamst! Du glaubtest an meine Noth, als du mir den Kopf mit beiden Händen hieltest, –

– ich hörte dich jammern 'man hat ihn zu wenig geliebt, zu wenig geliebt!' Daß ich dich soweit betrog, darüber frohlockte inwendig meine Bosheit."

"Du magst Feinere betrogen haben als mich, sagte Zarathustra hart. Ich bin nicht auf der Hut vor Betrügern, ich muss ohne Vorsicht sein: so will es mein Loos.

Du aber – mußt betrügen: so weit kenne ich dich! Du mußt immer zwei= drei= vier= und fünfdeutig sein! Auch was du jetzt bekanntest, war mir lange nicht wahr und nicht falsch genug!

Du schlimmer Falschmünzer, wie könntest du anders! Deine Krankheit würdest du noch schminken, wenn du dich deinem Arzte nackt zeigtest.

So schminktest du eben vor mir deine Lüge, als du sprachst: ‚ich trieb's also nur zum Spiele!' Es war auch Ernst darin, du bist Etwas von einem Büsser des Geistes!

Ich errathe dich wohl: du wurdest der Bezauberer Aller, aber gegen dich hast du keine Lüge und List mehr übrig, – du selber bist dir entzaubert!

Du erntetest den Ekel ein, als deine Eine Wahrheit. Kein Wort ist mehr an dir echt, aber dein Mund: nämlich der Ekel, der an deinem Munde klebt." – –

– "Wer bist du doch! schrie hier der alte Zauberer mit einer trotzigen Stimme, wer darf also zu mir reden, dem Grössten, der heute lebt?" – und ein grüner Blitz schoss aus seinem Auge nach Zarathustra. Aber gleich darauf verwandelte er sich und sagte traurig:

"O Zarathustra, ich bin's müde, es ekelt mich meiner Künste, ich bin nicht gross, was verstelle ich mich! Aber, du weißt es wohl – ich suchte nach Grösse!

Einen grossen Menschen wollte ich vorstellen und überredete Viele: aber diese Lüge gieng über meine Kraft. An ihr zerbreche ich.

O Zarathustra, Alles ist Lüge an mir; aber daß ich zerbreche – dies mein Zerbrechen ist echt!" –

"Es ehrt dich, sprach Zarathustra düster und zur Seite niederblickend, es ehrt dich, daß du nach Grösse suchtest, aber es verräth dich auch. Du bist nicht gross.

Du schlimmer alter Zauberer, das ist dein Bestes und Redlichstes, was ich an dir ehre, daß du deiner müde wurdest und es aussprachst: 'ich bin nicht gross.'

Darin ehre ich dich als einen Büsser des Geistes: und wenn auch nur für einen Hauch und Husch, diesen Einen Augenblick warst du – echt.

Aber sprich, was suchst du hier in meinen Wäldern und Felsen? Und wenn du mir dich in den Weg legtest, welche Probe wolltest du von mir? –

– wess versuchtest du mich?" –

Also sprach Zarathustra, und seine Augen funkelten. Der alte Zauberer schwieg eine Weile, dann sagte er: "Versuchte ich dich? Ich – suche nur.

O Zarathustra, ich suche einen Echten, Rechten, Einfachen, Eindeutigen, einen Menschen aller Redlichkeit, ein Gefäss der Weisheit, einen Heiligen der Erkenntnis, einen grossen Menschen!

Weißt du es denn nicht, O Zarathustra? Ich suche Zarathustra."

– Und hier entstand ein langes Stillschweigen zwischen Beiden; Zarathustra aber versank tief hinein in sich selber, also daß er die Augen schloss. Dann aber, zu seinem Unterredner zurückkehrend, ergriff er die Hand des Zauberers und sprach, voller Artigkeit und Arglist:

"Wohlan! Dort hinauf führt der Weg, da liegt die Höhle Zarathustras. In ihr darfst du suchen, wen du finden möchtest.

Und frage meine Thiere um Rath, meinen Adler und meine Schlange: die sollen dir suchen helfen. Meine Höhle aber ist gross.

Der Zauberer

Ich selber freilich – ich sah noch keinen grossen Menschen. Was gross ist, dafür ist das Auge der Feinsten heute grob. Es ist das Reich des Pöbels.

So Manchen fand ich schon, der streckte und blähte sich, und das Volk schrie: 'Seht da, einen grossen Menschen!' Aber was helfen alle Blasebälge! Zuletzt fährt der Wind heraus.

Zuletzt platzt ein Frosch, der sich zu lange aufblies: da fährt der Wind heraus. Einem Geschwollnen in den Bauch stechen, das heisse ich eine brave Kurzweil. Hört das, ihr Knaben!

Dies Heute ist des Pöbels: wer weiss da noch, was gross, was klein ist! Wer suchte da mit Glück nach Grösse! Ein Narr allein: den Narren glückt's.

Du suchst nach grossen Menschen, du wunderlicher Narr? Wer lehrte's dich? ist heute dazu die Zeit? O du schlimmer Sucher, was – versuchst du mich?" – –

Also sprach Zarathustra, getrösteten Herzens, und gierig lachend seines Wegs fürbass.

Ausser Dienst

Nicht lange aber, nachdem Zarathustra sich von dem Zauberer losgemacht hatte, sahe er wiederum Jemanden am Wege sitzen, den er gieng, nämlich einen schwarzen langen Mann mit einem hageren Bleichgesicht: der verdross ihn gewaltig. "Wehe, sprach er zu seinem Herzen, da, sitzt vermummte Trübsal, das dünkt mich von der Art der Priester: was wollen die in meinem Reiche?

Wie! Kaum bin ich jenem Zauberer entronnen: muss mir da wieder ein anderer Schwarzkünstler über den Weg laufen, –

– irgend ein Hexenmeister mit Handauflegen, ein dunkler Wunderthäter von Gottes Gnaden, ein gesalbter Welt-Verleumder, den der Teufel holen möge!

Aber der Teufel ist nie am Platze, wo er am Platze wäre: immer kommt er zu spät, dieser vermaledeite Zwerg und Klumpfuss!"

– Also fluchte Zarathustra ungeduldig in seinem Herzen und gedachte, wie er abgewandten Blicks an dem schwarzen Manne vorüberschlüpfe: aber siehe, es kam anders. Im gleichen Augenblicke nämlich hatte ihn schon der Sitzende erblickt; und nicht unähnlich einem Solchen, dem ein unvermuthetes Glück zustösst, sprang er auf und gieng auf Zarathustra los.

"Wer du auch bist, du Wandersmann, sprach er, hilf einem Verirrten, einem Suchenden, einem alten Manne, der hier leicht zu Schaden kommt!

Diese Welt hier ist mir fremd und fern, auch hörte ich wilde Thiere heulen; und Der, welcher mir hätte Schutz bieten können, der ist selber nicht mehr.

Ich suchte den letzten frommen Menschen, einen Heiligen und Einsiedler, der allein in seinem Walde noch Nichts davon gehört hatte, was alle Welt heute weiss."

"Was weiss heute alle Welt? fragte Zarathustra. Etwa dies, daß der alte Gott nicht mehr lebt, an den alle Welt einst geglaubt hat?"

"Du sagst es, antwortete der alte Mann betrübt. Und ich diente diesem alten Gotte bis zu seiner letzten Stunde.

Nun aber bin ich ausser Dienst, ohne Herrn, und doch nicht frei, auch keine Stunde mehr lustig, es sei denn in Erinnerungen.

Ausser Dienst

Dazu stieg ich in diese Berge, daß ich endlich wieder ein Fest mir machte, wie es einem alten Papste und Kirchen-Vater zukommt: denn wisse, ich bin der letzte Papst! – ein Fest frommer Erinnerungen und Gottesdienste.

Nun aber ist er selber todt, der frömmste Mensch, jener Heilige im Walde, der seinen Gott beständig mit Singen und Brummen lobte.

Ihn selber fand ich nicht mehr, als ich seine Hütte fand, – wohl aber zwei Wölfe darin, welche um seinen Tod heulten – denn alle Thiere liebten ihn. Da lief ich davon.

Kam ich also umsonst in diese Wälder und Berge? Da entschloss sich mein Herz, daß ich einen Anderen suchte, den Frömmsten aller Derer, die nicht an Gott glauben –, daß ich Zarathustra suchte!"

Also sprach der Greis und blickte scharfen Auges Den an, welcher vor ihm stand; Zarathustra aber ergriff die Hand des alten Papstes und betrachtete sie lange mit Bewunderung.

"Siehe da, du Ehrwürdiger, sagte er dann, welche schöne und lange Hand! Das ist die Hand eines Solchen, der immer Segen ausgetheilt hat. Nun aber hält sie Den fest, welchen du suchst, mich, Zarathustra.

Ich bin's, der gottlose Zarathustra, der da spricht: wer ist gottloser als ich, daß ich mich seiner Unterweisung freue?"

– Also sprach Zarathustra und durchbohrte mit seinen Blicken die Gedanken und Hintergedanken des alten Papstes. Endlich begann dieser:

"Wer ihn am meisten liebte und besass, der hat ihn nun am meisten auch verloren –:

– siehe, ich selber bin wohl von uns Beiden jetzt der Gottlosere? Aber wer könnte daran sich freuen!" –

"Du dientest ihm bis zuletzt, fragte Zarathustra nachdenklich, nach einem tiefen Schweigen, du weißt, wie er starb? ist es wahr, was man spricht, daß ihn das Mitleiden erwürgte,

– daß er es sah, wie der Mensch am Kreuze hieng, und es nicht ertrug, daß die Liebe zum Menschen seine Hölle und zuletzt sein Tod wurde?" –

Der alte Papst aber antwortete nicht, sondern blickte scheu und mit einem schmerzlichen und düsteren Ausdrucke zur Seite.

"Lass ihn fahren, sagte Zarathustra nach einem langen Nachdenken, indem er immer noch dem alten Manne gerade in's Auge blickte.

Lass ihn fahren, er ist dahin. Und ob es dich auch ehrt, daß du diesem Todten nur Gutes nachredest, so weißt du so gut als ich, wer er war; und daß er wunderliche Wege gieng."

"Unter drei Augen gesprochen, sagte erheitert der alte Papst (denn er war auf Einem Auge blind), in Dingen Gottes bin ich aufgeklärter als Zarathustra selber – und darf es sein.

Meine Liebe diente ihm lange Jahre, mein Wille gierig allem seinen Willen nach. Ein guter Diener aber weiss Alles, und Mancherlei auch, was sein Herr sich selbst verbirgt.

Es war ein verborgener Gott, voller Heimlichkeit. Wahrlich zu einem Sohne sogar kam er nicht anders als auf Schleichwegen. An der Thür seines Glaubens steht der Ehebruch.

Wer ihn als einen Gott der Liebe preist, denkt nicht hoch genug von der Liebe selber. Wollte dieser Gott nicht auch Richter sein? Aber der Liebende liebt jenseits von Lohn und Vergeltung.

Als er jung war, dieser Gott aus dem Morgenlande, da war er hart und rachsüchtig und erbaute sich eine Hölle zum Ergötzen seiner Lieblinge.

Endlich aber wurde er alt und weich und mürbe und mitleidig, einem Grossvater ähnlicher als einem Vater, am ähnlichsten aber einer wackeligen alten Grossmutter.

Da sass er, welk, in seinem Ofenwinkel, härmte sich ob seiner schwachen Beine, weltmüde, willensmüde, und erstickte eines Tags an seinem allzugrossen Mitleiden." –

"Du alter Papst, sagte hier Zarathustra dazwischen, hast du Das mit Augen angesehn? Es könnte wohl so abgegangen sein: so, und auch anders. Wenn Götter sterben, sterben sie immer viele Arten Todes.

Aber wohlan! So oder so, so und so – er ist dahin! Er gieng meinen Ohren und Augen wider den Geschmack, Schlimmeres möchte ich ihm nicht nachsagen.

Ich liebe Alles, was hell blickt und redlich redet. Aber er – du weißt es ja, du alter Priester, es war Etwas von deiner Art an ihm, von Priester-Art – er war vieldeutig.

Er war auch undeutlich. Was hat er uns darob gezürnt, dieser Zornschnauber, daß wir ihn schlecht verstünden! Aber warum sprach er nicht reinlicher?

Und lag es an unsern Ohren, warum gab er uns Ohren, die ihn schlecht hörten? War Schlamm in unsern Ohren, wohlan! wer legte ihn hinein?

Zu Vieles mißrieth ihm, diesem Töpfer, der nicht ausgelernt hatte! Daß er aber Rache an seinen Töpfen und Geschöpfen nahm, dafür daß sie ihm schlecht geriethen, – das war eine Sünde wider den guten Geschmack.

Es giebt auch in der Frömmigkeit guten Geschmack: der sprach endlich 'Fort mit einem solchen Gotte! Lieber keinen Gott, lieber auf eigne Faust Schicksal machen, lieber Narr sein, lieber selber Gott sein!'"

– "Was höre ich! sprach hier der alte Papst mit gespitzten Ohren; O Zarathustra, du bist frömmer als du glaubst, mit einem solchen Unglauben! Irgend ein Gott in dir bekehrte dich zu deiner Gottlosigkeit.

Ist es nicht deine Frömmigkeit selber, die dich nicht mehr an einen Gott glauben läßt? Und deine übergrosse Redlichkeit wird dich auch noch jenseits von Gut und Böse wegführen!

Siehe, doch, was blieb dir aufgespart? Du hast Augen und Hand und Mund, die sind zum Segnen vorher bestimmt seit Ewigkeit. Man segnet nicht mit der Hand allein.

In deiner Nähe, ob du schon der Gottloseste sein willst, wittere ich einen heimlichen Weih- und Wohlgeruch von langen Segnungen: mir wird wohl und wehe dabei.

Lass mich deinen Gast sein, O Zarathustra, für eine einzige Nacht! Nirgends auf Erden wird es mir jetzt wohler als bei dir!" –

"Amen! So soll es sein! sprach Zarathustra mit grosser Verwunderung, dort hinauf führt der Weg, da liegt die Höhle Zarathustras.

Gerne, fürwahr, würde ich dich selber dahin geleiten, du Ehrwürdiger, denn ich liebe alle frommen Menschen. Aber jetzt ruft mich eilig ein Nothschrei weg von dir.

In meinem Bereiche soll mir Niemand zu Schaden kommen; meine Höhle ist ein guter Hafen. Und am liebsten möchte ich jedweden Traurigen wieder auf festes Land und feste Beine stellen.

Wer aber nähme dir deine Schwermuth von der Schulter? Dazu bin ich zu schwach. Lange, wahrlich, möchten wir warten, bis dir Einer deinen Gott wieder aufweckt.

Dieser alte Gott nämlich lebt nicht mehr: der ist gründlich todt." –

Also sprach Zarathustra.

Der häßlichste Mensch

Und wieder liefen Zarathustras Füsse durch Berge und Wälder, und seine Augen suchten und suchten, aber nirgends war Der zu sehen, welchen sie sehn wollten, der grosse Nothleidende und Nothschreiende. Auf dem ganzen Wege aber frohlockte er in seinem Herzen und war dankbar. "Welche guten Dinge, sprach er, schenkte mir doch dieser Tag, zum Entgelt, daß er schlimm begann! Welche seltsamen Unterredner fand ich!

An deren Worten will ich lange nun kauen gleich als an guten Körnern; klein soll mein Zahn sie mahlen und malmen, bis sie mir wie Milch in die Seele fliessen!" –

Als aber der Weg wieder um einen Felsen bog, veränderte sich mit Einem Male die Landschaft, und Zarathustra trat in ein Reich des Todes. Hier starrten schwarze und rothe Klippen empor: kein Gras, kein Baum, keine Vogelstimme. Es war nämlich ein Thal, welches alle Thiere mieden, auch die Raubthiere-, nur daß eine Art hässlicher, dicker, grüner Schlangen, wenn sie alt wurden, hierher kamen, um zu sterben. Darum nannten dies Thal die Hirten: Schlangen-Tod.

Zarathustra aber versank in eine schwarze Erinnerung, denn ihm war, als habe er schon einmal in diesem Thal gestanden. Und vieles Schwere legte sich ihm über den Sinn: also, daß er langsam gieng und immer langsamer und endlich still stand. Da aber sahe er, als er die Augen aufthat, Etwas, das am Wege sass, gestaltet wie ein Mensch und kaum wie ein Mensch, etwas Unaussprechliches. Und mit Einem Schlage überfiel Zarathustra die grosse Scham darob, daß er so Etwas mit den Augen angesehn habe: erröthend bis hinauf an sein weisses Haar, wandte er den Blick ab und hob den Fuss, daß er diese schlimme Stelle verlasse. Da aber wurde die todte Öde laut: vom Boden auf nämlich quoll es gurgelnd und röchelnd, wie Wasser Nachts durch verstopfte Wasser-Röhren gurgelt und röchelt; und zuletzt wurde daraus eine Menschen-Stimme und Menschen-Rede. – die lautete also:

"Zarathustra! Zarathustra! Rathe mein Räthsel! Sprich, sprich! Was ist die Rache am Zeugen?

Ich locke dich zurück, hier ist glattes Eis! Sieh zu, sieh zu, ob dein Stolz sich hier nicht die Beine bricht!

Du dünkst dich weise, du stolzer Zarathustra! So rathe doch das Räthsel, du harter Nüsseknacker, – das Räthsel, das ich bin! So sprich doch – wer bin ich!"
– Als aber Zarathustra diese Worte gehört hatte, – was glaubt ihr wohl, daß sich da mit seiner Seele zutrug? Das Mitleiden fiel ihn an; und er sank mit Einem Male nieder, wie ein Eichbaum, der lange vielen Holzschlägern widerstanden hat, – schwer, plötzlich, zum Schrecken selber für Die, welche ihn fällen wollten. Aber schon stand er wieder vom Boden auf, und sein Antlitz wurde hart.

"Ich erkenne dich wohl, sprach er mit einer erzenen Stimme: du bist der Mörder Gottes! Lass mich gehn.

Du ertrugst Den nicht, der dich sah, – der dich immer und durch und durch sah, du hässlichster Mensch! Du nahmst Rache an diesem Zeugen!"

Also sprach Zarathustra und wollte davon; aber der Unaussprechliche faßte nach einem Zipfel seines Gewandes und begann von Neuem zu gurgeln und nach Worten zu suchen. "Bleib!" sagte er endlich –

– "bleib! Geh nicht vorüber! Ich errieth, welche Axt dich zu Boden schlug: Heil dir, O Zarathustra, daß du wieder stehst!

Du erriethest, ich weiss es gut, wie Dem zu Muthe ist, der ihn tödtete, – dem Mörder Gottes. Bleib! Setze dich her zu mir, es ist nicht umsonst.

Zu wem wollte ich, wenn nicht zu dir? Bleib, setze dich! Blicke mich aber nicht an! Ehre also – meine Hässlichkeit!

Sie verfolgen mich: nun bist du meine letzte Zuflucht. Nicht mit ihrem Hasse, nicht mit ihren Häschern: – oh solcher Verfolgung würde ich spotten und stolz und froh sein!

War nicht aller Erfolg bisher bei den Gut-Verfolgten? Und wer gut verfolgt, lernt leicht folgen: – ist er doch einmal – hinterher! Aber ihr Mitleid ist's –

– ihr Mitleid ist's, vor dem ich flüchte und dir zuflüchte. O Zarathustra, schütze mich, du meine letzte Zuflucht, du Einziger, der mich errieth:

– du erriethest, wie Dem zu Muthe ist, welcher ihn tödtete. Bleib! Und willst du gehn, du Ungeduldiger: geh nicht den Weg, den ich kam. Der Weg ist schlecht.

Zürnst du mir, daß ich zu lange schon rede-rade-breche? Daß ich schon dir rathe? Aber wisse, ich bin's, der hässlichste Mensch,

– der auch die grössten schwersten Füsse hat. Wo ich gieng, ist der Weg schlecht. Ich trete alle Wege todt und zu Schanden.

Daß du aber an mir vorübergiengst, schweigend; daß du erröthetest, ich sah es wohl: daran erkannte ich dich als Zarathustra. Jedweder Andere hätte mir sein Almosen zugeworfen, sein Mitleiden, mit Blick und Rede. Aber dazu – bin ich nicht Bettler genug, das erriethest du –

– dazu bin ich zu reich, reich an Grossem, an Furchtbarem, am Hässlichsten, am Unaussprechlichsten! Deine Scham, O Zarathustra, ehrte mich!

Mit Noth kam ich heraus aus dem Gedräng der Mitleidigen, – daß ich den Einzigen fände, der heute lehrt 'Mitleiden ist zudringlich' – dich, O Zarathustra!

– sei es eines Gottes, sei es der Menschen Mitleiden: Mitleiden geht gegen die Scham. Und nicht-helfen-wollen kann vornehmer sein als jene Tugend, die zuspringt.

Das aber heißt heute Tugend selber bei allen kleinen Leuten, das Mitleiden: – die haben keine Ehrfurcht vor grossem Unglück, vor grosser Hässlichkeit, vor grossem Mißrathen.

Über diese Alle blicke ich hinweg, wie ein Hund über die Rücken wimmelnder Schafheerden wegblickt. Es sind kleine wohlwollige wohlwillige graue Leute.

Wie ein Reiher verachtend über flache Teiche wegblickt, mit zurückgelegtem Kopfe: so blicke ich über das Gewimmel grauer kleiner Wellen und Willen und Seelen weg.

Zu lange hat man ihnen Recht gegeben, diesen kleinen Leuten: so gab man ihnen endlich auch die Macht – nun lehren sie: 'gut ist nur, was kleine Leute gut heissen.'

Und 'Wahrheit' heißt heute, was der Prediger sprach, der selber aus ihnen herkam, jener wunderliche Heilige und Fürsprecher der kleinen Leute, welcher von sich zeugte 'ich – bin die Wahrheit.'

Dieser Unbescheidne macht nun lange schon den kleinen Leuten den Kamm hoch schwellen – er, der keinen kleinen Irrthum lehrte, als er lehrte 'ich – bin die Wahrheit.'

Ward einem Unbescheidnen jemals höflicher geantwortet? – Du aber, O Zarathustra, giengst an ihm vorüber und sprachst: 'Nein! Nein! Dreimal Nein!'

Du warntest vor seinem Irrthum, du warntest als der Erste vor dem Mitleiden – nicht Alle, nicht Keinen, sondern dich und deine Art.

Der häßlichste Mensch

Du schämst dich an der Scham des grossen Leidenden; und wahrlich, wann du sprichst 'von dem Mitleiden her kommt eine grosse Wolke, habt Acht, ihr Menschen!'
– wann du lehrst 'alle Schaffenden sind hart, alle grosse Liebe ist über ihrem Mitleiden': O Zarathustra, wie gut dünkst du mich eingelernt auf Wetter-Zeichen!
Du selber aber – warne dich selber auch vor deinem Mitleiden! Denn Viele sind zu dir unterwegs, viele Leidende, Zweifelnde, Verzweifelnde, Ertrinkende, Frierende –
Ich warne dich auch vor mir. Du erriethest mein bestes, schlimmstes Räthsel, mich selber und was ich that. Ich kenne die Axt, die dich fällt.
Aber er – mußte sterben: er sah mit Augen, welche Alles sahn, – er sah des Menschen Tiefen und Gründe, alle seine verhehlte Schmach und Hässlichkeit.
Sein Mitleiden kannte keine Scham: er kroch in meine schmutzigsten Winkel. Dieser Neugierigste, Über-Zudringliche, Über-Mitleidige mußte sterben.
Er sah immer mich: an einem solchen Zeugen wollte ich Rache haben – oder selber nicht leben.
Der Gott, der Alles sah, auch den Menschen: dieser Gott mußte sterben! Der Mensch erträgt es nicht, daß solch ein Zeuge lebt."

Also, sprach der hässlichste Mensch. Zarathustra aber erhob sich und schickte sich an fortzugehn: denn ihn fröstelte bis in seine Eingeweide.
"Du Unaussprechlicher, sagte er, du warntest mich vor deinem Wege. Zum Danke dafür lobe ich dir den meinen. Siehe, dort hinauf liegt die Höhle Zarathustras.
Meine Höhle ist gross und tief und hat viele Winkel; da findet der Versteckteste sein Versteck.
Und dicht bei ihr sind hundert Schlüpfe und Schliche für kriechendes, flatterndes und springendes Gethier.
Du Ausgestossener, der du dich selber ausstießest, du willst nicht unter Menschen und Menschen-Mitleid wohnen? Wohlan, so thu's mir gleich! So lernst du auch von mir; nur der Thäter lernt.
Und rede zuerst und =nächst mit meinen Thieren! Das stolzeste Thier und das klügste Thier – die möchten uns Beiden wohl die rechten Rathgeber sein!" – –

Der häßlichste Mensch

Also sprach Zarathustra und gieng seiner Wege, nachdenklicher und langsamer noch als zuvor: denn er fragte sich Vieles und wußte sich nicht leicht zu antworten.

"Wie arm ist doch der Mensch! dachte er in seinem Herzen, wie hässlich, wie röchelnd, wie voll verborgener Scham!

Man sagt mir, daß der Mensch sich selber liebe: ach, wie gross muss diese Selber-Liebe sein! Wie viel Verachtung hat sie wider sich!

Auch dieser da liebte sich, wie er sich verachtete, – ein grosser Liebender ist er mir und ein grosser Verächter.

Keinen fand ich noch, der sich tiefer verachtet hätte: auch Das ist Höhe. Wehe, war Der vielleicht der höhere Mensch, dessen Schrei ich hörte?

Ich liebe die grossen Verachtenden. Der Mensch aber ist Etwas, das überwunden werden muss." – –

Der freiwillige Bettler

Als Zarathustra den hässlichsten Menschen verlassen hatte, fror ihn, und er fühlte sich einsam: es gieng ihm nämlich vieles Kalte und Einsame durch die Sinne, also, daß darob auch seine Glieder kälter wurden. Indem er aber weiter und weiter stieg, hinauf, hinab, bald an grünen Weiden vorbei, aber auch über wilde steinichte Lager, wo ehedem wohl ein ungeduldiger Bach sich zu Bett gelegt hatte,- da wurde ihm mit Einem Male wieder wärmer und herzlicher zu Sinne.

"Was geschah mir doch? fragte er sich, etwas Warmes und Lebendiges erquickt mich, das muss in meiner Nähe sein.

Schon bin ich weniger allein; unbewußte Gefährten und Brüder schweifen um mich, ihr warmer Athem rührt an meine Seele."

Als er aber um sich spähete und nach den Tröstern seiner Einsamkeit suchte: siehe, da waren es Kühe, welche auf einer Anhöhe bei einander standen; deren Nähe und Geruch hatten sein Herz erwärmt. Diese Kühe aber schienen mit Eifer einem Redenden zuzuhören und gaben nicht auf Den Acht, der herankam. Wie aber Zarathustra ganz in ihrer Nähe war, hörte er deutlich, daß eine Menschen=Stimme aus der Mitte der Kühe heraus redete; und ersichtlich hatten sie allesammt ihre Köpfe dem Redenden zugedreht.

Da sprang Zarathustra mit Eifer hinauf und drängte die Thiere auseinander, denn er fürchtete, daß hier jemandem ein Leids geschehn sei, welchem schwerlich das Mitleid von Kühen abhelfen mochte. Aber darin hatte er sich getäuscht; denn siehe, da sass ein Mensch auf der Erde und schien den Thieren zuzureden, daß sie keine Scheu vor ihm haben sollten, ein friedfertiger Mensch und Berg=Prediger, aus dessen Augen die Güte selber predigte. "Was suchst du hier?" rief Zarathustra mit Befremden.

"Was ich hier suche? antwortete er: das Selbe, was du suchst, du Störenfried! nämlich das Glück auf Erden.

Dazu aber möchte ich von diesen Kühen lernen. Denn, weißt du wohl, einen halben Morgen schon rede ich ihnen zu, und eben wollten sie mir Bescheid geben. Warum doch störst du sie?

So wir nicht umkehren und werden wie die Kühe, so kommen wir nicht in das Himmelreich. Wir sollten ihnen nämlich Eins ablernen: das Wiederkäuen.

Und wahrlich, wenn der Mensch auch die ganze Welt gewönne und lernte das Eine nicht, das Wiederkäuen: was hülfe es! Er würde nicht seine Trübsal los
– seine grosse Trübsal: die aber heißt heute Ekel. Wer hat heute von Ekel nicht Herz, Mund und Augen voll? Auch du! Auch du! Aber siehe doch diese Kühe an!" –

Also sprach der Berg-Prediger und wandte dann seinen eignen Blick Zarathustra zu, – denn bisher hieng er mit Liebe an den Kühen –: da aber verwandelte er sich. "Wer ist das, mit dem ich rede? rief er erschreckt und sprang vom Boden empor.

Dies ist der Mensch ohne Ekel, dies ist Zarathustra selber, der Überwinder des grossen Ekels, dies ist das Auge, dies ist der Mund, dies ist das Herz Zarathustras selber."

Und indem er also sprach, küßte er Dem, zu welchem er redete, die Hände, mit überströmenden Augen, und gebärdete sich ganz als Einer, dem ein kostbares Geschenk und Kleinod unversehens vom Himmel fällt. Die Kühe aber schauten dem Allen zu und wunderten sich.

"Sprich nicht von mir, du Wunderlicher! Lieblicher! sagte Zarathustra und wehrte seiner Zärtlichkeit, sprich mir erst von dir! Bist du nicht der freiwillige Bettler, der einst einen grossen Reichthum von sich warf, –

– der sich seines Reichthums schämte und der Reichen, und zu den Ärmsten floh, daß er ihnen seine Fülle und sein Herz schenke? Aber sie nahmen ihn nicht an."

"Aber sie nahmen mich nicht an, sagte der freiwillige Bettler, du weißt es ja. So gieng ich endlich zu den Thieren und zu diesen Kühen."

"Da lerntest du, unterbrach Zarathustra den Redenden, wie es schwerer ist, recht geben als recht nehmen, und daß gut schenken eine Kunst ist und die letzte listigste Meister-Kunst der Güte."

"Sonderlich heutzutage, antwortete der freiwillige Bettler: heute nämlich, wo alles Niedrige aufständisch ward und scheu und auf seine Art hoffährtig: nämlich auf Pöbel-Art.

Denn es kam die Stunde, du weißt es ja, für den grossen schlimmen langen langsamen Pöbel- und Sklaven-Aufstand: der wächst und wächst!

Nun empört die Niedrigen alles Wohlthun und kleine Weggeben; und die Überreichen mögen auf der Hut sein!

Wer heute gleich bauchichten Flaschen tröpfelt aus allzuschmalen Hälsen: – solchen Flaschen bricht man heute gern den Hals.

Der freiwillige Bettler

Lüsterne Gier, gallichter Neid, vergrämte Rachsucht, Pöbel-Stolz: das sprang mir Alles in's Gesicht. Es ist nicht mehr wahr, dass die Armen selig sind. Das Himmelreich aber ist bei den Kühen."

"Und warum ist es nicht bei den Reichen?" fragte Zarathustra versuchend, während er den Kühen wehrte, die den Friedfertigen zutraulich anschnaufelten.

"Was versuchst du mich?" antwortete dieser. "Du weisst es selber besser noch als ich. Was trieb mich doch zu den Ärmsten, O Zarathustra? War es nicht der Ekel vor unsern Reichsten?

– vor den Sträflingen des Reichthums, welche sich ihren Vortheil aus jedem Kehricht auflesen, mit kalten Augen, geilen Gedanken, vor diesem Gesindel, das gen Himmel stinkt,

– vor diesem vergüldeten verfälschten Pöbel, dessen Väter Langfinger oder Aasvögel oder Lumpensammler waren, mit Weibern willfährig, lüstern, vergesslich: – sie haben's nämlich alle nicht weit zur Hure –

Pöbel oben, Pöbel unten! Was ist heute noch 'Arm' und 'Reich'! Diesen Unterschied verlernte ich, – da floh ich davon, weiter, immer weiter, bis ich zu diesen Kühen kam."

Also sprach der Friedfertige und schnaufte selber und schwitzte bei seinen Worten: also dass die Kühe sich von Neuem wunderten. Zarathustra aber sah ihm immer mit Lächeln in's Gesicht, als er so hart redete, und schüttelte dazu schweigend den Kopf.

"Du thust dir Gewalt an, du Berg-Prediger, wenn du solche harte Worte brauchst. Für solche Härte wuchs dir nicht der Mund, nicht das Auge.

Auch, wie mich dünkt, dein Magen selber nicht: dem widersteht all solches Zürnen und Hassen und Überschäumen. Dein Magen will sanftere Dinge: du bist kein Fleischer.

Vielmehr dünkst du mich ein Pflanzer und Wurzelmann. Vielleicht malmst du Körner. Sicherlich aber bist du fleischlichen Freuden abhold und liebst den Honig."

"Du erriethst mich gut, antwortete der freiwillige Bettler, mit erleichtertem Herzen. Ich liebe den Honig, ich malme auch Körner, denn ich suchte, was lieblich mundet und reinen Athem macht:

– auch was lange Zeit braucht, ein Tag- und Maul-Werk für sanfte Müssiggänger und Tagediebe.

Am weitesten freilich brachten es diese Kühe: die erfanden sich das Wiederkäuen und In-der-Sonne-Liegen. Auch enthalten sie sich aller schweren Gedanken, welche das Herz blähn."

– "Wohlan! sagte Zarathustra: du solltest auch meine Thiere sehn, meinen Adler und meine Schlange, – ihres Gleichen giebt es heute nicht auf Erden.

Siehe, dorthin führt der Weg zu meiner Höhle: sei diese Nacht ihr Gast. Und rede mit meinen Thieren vom Glück der Thiere, –

– bis ich selber heimkomme. Denn jetzt ruft ein Nothschrei Mich eilig weg von dir. Auch findest du neuen Honig bei mir, eisfrischen Waben-Goldhonig: den iss!

Jetzt aber nimm flugs Abschied von deinen Kühen, du Wunderlicher! Lieblicher! ob es dir schon schwer werden mag. Denn es sind deine wärmsten Freunde und Lehrmeister!" –

"– Einen ausgenommen, den ich noch lieber habe, antwortete der freiwillige Bettler. Du selber bist gut und besser noch als eine Kuh, O Zarathustra!"

"Fort, fort mit dir! du arger Schmeichler! schrie Zarathustra mit Bosheit, was verdirbst du mich mit solchem Lob und Schmeichel-Honig?"

"Fort, fort von mir!" schrie er noch einmal und schwang seinen Stock nach dem zärtlichen Bettler: der aber lief hurtig davon.

Der Schatten

Kaum aber war der freiwillige Bettler davongelaufen und Zarathustra wieder mit sich allein, da hörte er hinter sich eine neue Stimme: die rief "Halt! Zarathustra! So warte doch! Ich bin's ja, O Zarathustra, ich, dein Schatten!" Aber Zarathustra wartete nicht, denn ein plötzlicher Verdruss überkam ihn ob des vielen Zudrangs und Gedrängs in seinen Bergen. "Wo ist meine Einsamkeit hin? sprach er.

Es wird mir wahrlich zu viel; dies Gebirge wimmelt, mein Reich ist nicht mehr von dieser Welt, ich brauche neue Berge.

Mein Schatten ruft mich? Was liegt an meinem Schatten! Mag er mir nachlaufen! ich – laufe ihm davon."

– Also sprach Zarathustra zu seinem Herzen und lief davon. Aber Der, welcher hinter ihm war, folgte ihm nach: so daß alsbald drei Laufende hinter einander her waren, nämlich voran der freiwillige Bettler, dann Zarathustra und zudritt und -hinterst sein Schatten. Nicht lange liefen sie so, da kam Zarathustra zur Besinnung über seine Thorheit und schüttelte mit Einem Rucke allen Verdruss und Überdruss von sich.

"Wie! sprach er, geschahen nicht von je die lächerlichsten Dinge bei uns alten Einsiedlern und Heiligen?

Wahrlich, meine Thorheit wuchs hoch in den Bergen! Nun höre ich sechs alte Narren-Beine hinter einander her klappern!

Darf aber Zarathustra sich wohl vor einem Schatten fürchten? Auch dünkt mich zu guterletzt, daß er längere Beine hat als ich."

Also sprach Zarathustra, lachend mit Augen und Eingeweiden, blieb stehen und drehte sich schnell herum – und siehe, fast warf er dabei seinen Nachfolger und Schatten zu Boden: so dicht schon folgte ihm derselbe auf den Fersen, und so schwach war er auch. Als er ihn nämlich mit Augen prüfte, erschrak er wie vor einem plötzlichen Gespenste: so dünn, schwärzlich, hohl und überlebt sah dieser Nachfolger aus.

"Wer bist du? fragte Zarathustra heftig, was treibst du hier? Und wesshalb heissest du dich meinen Schatten? Du gefällst mir nicht."

"Vergieb mir, antwortete der Schatten, daß ich's bin; und wenn ich dir nicht gefalle, wohlan, O Zarathustra! darin lobe ich dich und deinen guten Geschmack.

Ein Wanderer bin ich, der viel schon hinter deinen Fersen her giang: immer unterwegs, aber ohne Ziel, auch ohne Heim: also daß mir wahrlich wenig zum ewigen Juden fehlt, es sei denn, daß ich nicht ewig, und auch nicht Jude bin.

Wie? Muss ich immerdar unterwegs sein? Von jedem Winde gewirbelt, unstät, fortgetrieben? O Erde, du wardst mir zu rund!

Auf jeder Oberfläche sass ich schon, gleich müdem Staube schlief ich ein auf Spiegeln und Fensterscheiben: Alles nimmt von mir, Nichts giebt, ich werde dünn, – fast gleiche ich einem Schatten.

Dir aber, O Zarathustra, flog und zog ich am längsten nach, und, verbarg ich mich schon vor dir, so war ich doch dein bester Schatten: wo du nur gesessen hast, sass ich auch.

Mit dir bin ich in fernsten, kältesten Welten umgegangen, einem Gespenste gleich, das freiwillig über Winterdächer und Schnee läuft.

Mit dir strebte ich in jedes Verbotene, Schlimmste, Fernste: und wenn irgend Etwas an mir Tugend ist, so ist es, daß ich vor keinem Verbote Furcht hatte.

Mit dir zerbrach ich, was je mein Herz verehrte, alle Grenzsteine und Bilder warf ich um, den gefährlichsten Wünschen lief ich nach, – wahrlich, über jedwedes Verbrechen lief ich einmal hinweg.

Mit dir verlernte ich den Glauben an Worte und Werthe und grosse Namen. Wenn der Teufel sich häutet, fällt da nicht auch sein Name ab? der ist nämlich auch Haut. Der Teufel selber ist vielleicht – Haut.

'Nichts ist wahr, Alles ist erlaubt': so sprach ich mir zu. In die kältesten Wasser stürzte ich mich, mit Kopf und Herzen. Ach, wie oft stand ich darob nackt als rother Krebs da!

Ach, wohin kam mir alles Gute und alle Scham und aller Glaube an die Guten! Ach, wohin ist jene verlogne Unschuld, die ich einst besass, die Unschuld der Guten und ihrer edlen Lügen!

Zu oft, wahrlich, folgte ich der Wahrheit dicht auf dem Fusse: da trat sie mir vor den Kopf. Manchmal meinte ich zu lügen, und siehe! da erst traf ich – die Wahrheit.

Zu Viel klärte sich mir auf: nun geht es mich Nichts mehr an. Nichts lebt mehr, das ich liebe, – wie sollte ich noch mich selber lieben?

'Leben, wie ich Lust habe, oder gar nicht leben': so will ich's, so will's auch der Heiligste. Aber, wehe! wie habe ich noch – Lust?

Habe ich – noch ein Ziel? Einen Hafen, nach dem mein Segel läuft?

Einen guten Wind? Ach, nur wer weiss, wohin er fährt, weiss auch, welcher Wind gut und sein Fahrwind ist.

Was blieb mir noch zurück? Ein Herz müde und frech; ein unstäter Wille; Flatter=Flügel; ein zerbrochnes Rückgrat.

Dies Suchen nach meinem Heim: O Zarathustra, weißt du wohl, dies Suchen war meine Heimsuchung, es frißt mich auf.

'Wo ist – mein Heim?' Darnach frage und suche und suchte ich, das fand ich nicht. Oh ewiges Überall, oh ewiges Nirgendwo, oh ewiges – Umsonst!"

Also sprach der Schatten, und Zarathustras Gesicht verlängerte sich bei seinen Worten. "Du bist mein Schatten! sagte er endlich, mit Traurigkeit.

Deine Gefahr ist keine kleine, du freier Geist und Wanderer! Du hast einen schlimmen Tag gehabt: sieh zu, daß dir nicht noch ein schlimmerer Abend kommt!

Solchen Unstäten, wie du, dünkt zuletzt auch ein Gefängniss selig. Sahst du je, wie eingefangne Verbrecher schlafen? Sie schlafen ruhig, sie geniessen ihre neue Sicherheit.

Hüte dich, daß dich nicht am Ende noch ein enger Glaube einfängt, ein harter, strenger Wahn! Dich nämlich verführt und versucht nunmehr Jegliches, das eng und fest ist.

Du hast das Ziel verloren: wehe, wie wirst du diesen Verlust verscherzen und verschmerzen? Damit – hast du auch den Weg verloren!

Du armer Schweifender, Schwärmender, du müder Schmetterling! willst du diesen Abend eine Rast und Heimstätte haben? So gehe hinauf zu meiner Höhle!

Dorthin führt der Weg zu meiner Höhle. Und jetzo will ich schnell wieder von dir davonlaufen. Schon liegt es wie ein Schatten auf mir.

Ich will allein laufen, daß es wieder hell um mich werde. Dazu muss ich noch lange lustig auf den Beinen sein. Des Abends aber wird bei mir – getanzt!" – –

Also sprach Zarathustra.

Mittags

Und Zarathustra lief und lief und fand Niemanden mehr und war allein und fand immer wieder sich und genoss und schlürfte seine Einsamkeit und dachte an gute Dinge, – stundenlang. Um die Stunde des Mittags aber, als die Sonne gerade über Zarathustras Haupte stand, kam er an einem alten krummen und knorrichten Baume vorbei, der von der reichen Liebe eines Weinstocks rings umarmt und vor sich selber verborgen war: von dem hiengen gelbe Trauben in Fülle dem Wandernden entgegen. Da gelüstete ihn, einen kleinen Durst zu löschen und sich eine Traube abzubrechen; als er aber schon den Arm dazu ausstreckte, da gelüstete ihn etwas Anderes noch mehr: nämlich sich neben den Baum niederzulegen, um die Stunde des vollkommnen Mittags, und zu schlafen.

Dies that Zarathustra; und sobald er auf dem Boden lag, in der Stille und Heimlichkeit des bunten Grases, hatte er auch schon seinen kleinen Durst vergessen und schlief ein. Denn, wie das Sprichwort Zarathustras sagt: Eins ist nothwendiger als das Andre. Nur dass seine Augen offen blieben: – sie wurden nämlich nicht satt, den Baum und die Liebe des Weinstocks zu sehn und zu preisen. Im Einschlafen aber sprach Zarathustra also zu seinem Herzen:

Still! Still! Ward die Welt nicht eben vollkommen? Was geschieht mir doch?

Wie ein zierlicher Wind, ungesehn, auf getäfeltem Meere tanzt, leicht, federleicht: so – tanzt der Schlaf auf mir.

Kein Auge drückt er mir zu, die Seele lässt er mir wach. Leicht ist er, wahrlich! federleicht.

Er überredet mich, ich weiss nicht wie?, er betupft mich innewendig mit schmeichelnder Hand, er zwingt mich. Ja, er zwingt mich, dass meine Seele sich ausstreckt: –

– wie sie mir lang und müde wird, meine wunderliche Seele! Kam ihr eines siebenten Tages Abend gerade am Mittage? Wandelte sie zu lange schon selig zwischen guten und reifen Dingen?

Sie streckt sich lang aus, lang, – länger! sie liegt stille, meine wunderliche Seele. Zu viel Gutes hat sie schon geschmeckt, diese goldene Traurigkeit drückt sie, sie verzieht den Mund.

Mittags

– Wie ein Schiff, das in seine stillste Bucht einlief: – nun lehnt es sich an die Erde, der langen Reisen müde und der ungewissen Meere. Ist die Erde nicht treuer?

Wie solch ein Schiff sich dem Lande anlegt, anschmiegt: – da genügt's, daß eine Spinne vom Lande her zu ihm ihren Faden spinnt. Keiner stärkeren Taue bedarf es da.

Wie solch ein müdes Schiff in der stillsten Bucht: so ruhe auch ich nun der Erde nahe, treu, zutrauend, wartend, mit den leisesten Fäden ihr angebunden.

O Glück! O Glück! Willst du wohl singen, O meine Seele? Du liegst im Grase. Aber das ist die heimliche feierliche Stunde, wo kein Hirt seine Flöte bläst.

Scheue dich! Heisser Mittag schläft auf den Fluren. Singe. nicht! Still! Die Welt ist vollkommen.

Singe nicht, du Gras-Geflügel, O meine Seele! Flüstere nicht einmal! Sieh doch – still! der alte Mittag schläft, er bewegt den Mund: trinkt er nicht eben einen Tropfen Glücks –

– einen alten braunen Tropfen goldenen Glücks, goldenen Weins? Es huscht über ihn hin, sein Glück lacht. So – lacht ein Gott. Still! –

– "Zum Glück, wie wenig genügt schon zum Glücke!" So sprach ich einst, und dünkte mich klug. Aber es war eine Lästerung: das lernte ich nun. Kluge Narren reden besser.

Das Wenigste gerade, das Leiseste, Leichteste, einer Eidechse Rascheln, ein Hauch, ein Husch, ein Augen-Blick – *Wenig* macht die Art des *besten* Glücks. Still!

– Was geschah mir: Horch! Flog die Zeit wohl davon? Falle ich nicht? Fiel ich nicht – horch! in den Brunnen der Ewigkeit?

– Was geschieht mir? Still! Es sticht mich – wehe – in's Herz? In's Herz! Oh zerbrich, zerbrich, Herz, nach solchem Glücke, nach solchem Stiche!

– Wie? Ward die Welt nicht eben vollkommen? Rund und reif? Oh des goldenen runden Reifs – wohin fliegt er wohl? Laufe ich ihm nach! Husch!

Still – – (und hier dehnte sich Zarathustra und fühlte, daß er schlafe.)

"Auf! sprach er zu sich selber, du Schläfer! Du Mittagsschläfer! Wohlan, wohlauf, ihr alten Beine! Zeit ist's und Überzeit, manch gut Stück Wegs blieb euch noch zurück –

Nun schlieft ihr euch aus, wie lange doch? Eine halbe Ewigkeit! Wohlan, wohlauf nun, mein altes Herz! Wie lange erst darfst du nach solchem Schlaf – dich auswachen?"

(Aber da schlief er schon von Neuem ein, und seine Seele sprach gegen ihn und wehrte sich und legte sich wieder hin) – "Lass mich doch! Still! Ward nicht die Welt eben vollkommen? Oh des goldnen runden Balls!" –
"Steh auf, sprach Zarathustra, du kleine Diebin, du Tagediebin! Wie? Immer noch sich strecken, gähnen, seufzen, hinunterfallen in tiefe Brunnen?

Wer bist du doch! O meine Seele!" (und hier erschrak er, denn ein Sonnenstrahl fiel vom Himmel herunter auf sein Gesicht)

"O Himmel über mir, sprach er seufzend und setzte sich aufrecht, du schaust mir zu? Du horchst meiner wunderlichen Seele zu?

Wann trinkst du diesen Tropfen Thaus, der auf alle Erden=Dinge niederfiel, – wann trinkst du diese wunderliche Seele –

– wann, Brunnen der Ewigkeit! du heiterer schauerlicher Mittags=Abgrund! wann trinkst du meine Seele in dich zurück?"

Also sprach Zarathustra und erhob sich von seinem Lager am Baume wie aus einer fremden Trunkenheit: und siehe, da stand die Sonne immer noch gerade über seinem Haupte. Es möchte aber Einer daraus mit Recht abnehmen, daß Zarathustra damals nicht lange geschlafen habe.

Die Begrüssung

Am späten Nachmittage war es erst, daß Zarathustra, nach langem umsonstigen Suchen und Umherstreifen, wieder zu seiner Höhle heimkam. Als er aber derselben gegenüberstand, nicht zwanzig Schritt mehr von ihr ferne, da geschah das, was er jetzt am wenigsten erwartete: von Neuem hörte er den grossen Nothschrei. Und, erstaunlich! dies Mal kam derselbige aus seiner eignen Höhle. Es war aber ein langer vielfältiger seltsamer Schrei, und Zarathustra unterschied deutlich, daß er sich aus vielen Stimmen zusammensetze: mochte er schon, aus der Ferne gehört, gleich dem Schrei aus einem einzigen Munde klingen.

Da sprang Zarathustra auf seine Höhle zu, und siehe! welches Schauspiel erwartete ihn erst nach diesem Hörspiele! Denn da sassen sie allesammt bei einander, an denen er des Tags vorübergegangen war: der König zur Rechten und der König zur Linken, der alte Zauberer, der Papst, der freiwillige Bettler, der Schatten, der Gewissenhafte des Geistes, der traurige Wahrsager und der Esel; der hässlichste Mensch aber hatte sich eine Krone aufgesetzt und zwei Purpurgürtel umgeschlungen, – denn er liebte es, gleich allen Hässlichen, sich zu verkleiden und schön zu thun. Inmitten aber dieser betrübten Gesellschaft stand der Adler Zarathustras, gesträubt und unruhig, denn er sollte auf zu Vieles antworten, wofür sein Stolz keine Antwort hatte; die kluge Schlange aber hieng um seinen Hals.

Dies Alles schaute Zarathustra mit grosser Verwunderung; dann prüfte er jeden Einzelnen seiner Gäste mit leutseliger Neugierde, las ihre Seelen ab und wunderte sich von Neuem. Inzwischen hatten sich die Versammelten von ihren Sitzen erhoben und warteten mit Ehrfurcht, daß Zarathustra reden werde. Zarathustra aber sprach also:

"Ihr Verzweifelnden! Ihr Wunderlichen! Ich hörte also euren Nothschrei? Und nun weiss ich auch, wo Der zu suchen ist, den ich umsonst heute suchte: der höhere Mensch –:

– in meiner eignen Höhle sitzt er, der höhere Mensch! Aber was wundere ich mich! Habe ich ihn nicht selber zu mir gelockt durch Honig-Opfer und listige Lockrufe meines Glücks?

Doch dünkt mir, ihr taugt euch schlecht zur Gesellschaft, ihr macht einander das Herz unwirsch, ihr Nothschreienden, wenn ihr hier beisammen sitzt? Es muss erst Einer kommen,

– Einer, der auch wieder lachen macht, ein guter fröhlicher Hanswurst, ein Tänzer und Wind und Wildfang, irgend ein alter Narr: – was dünket euch?

Vergebt mir doch, ihr Verzweifelnden, dass ich vor euch mit solch kleinen Worten rede, unwürdig, wahrlich!, solcher Gäste! Aber ihr errathet nicht, was mein Herz muthwillig macht: –

– ihr selber thut es und euer Anblick, vergebt es mir! Jeder nämlich wird muthig, der einem Verzweifelnden zuschaut. Einem Verzweifelnden zuzusprechen – dazu dünkt sich jeder stark genug.

Mir selber gabt ihr diese Kraft, – eine gute Gabe, meine hohen Gäste! Ein rechtschaffnes Gastgeschenk! Wohlan, so zürnt nun nicht, dass ich euch auch vom Meinigen anbiete.

Dies hier ist mein Reich und meine Herrschaft: was aber mein ist, für diesen Abend und diese Nacht soll es euer sein. Meine Thiere sollen euch dienen: meine Höhle sei eure Ruhestatt!

Bei mir zu Heim-und-Hause soll Keiner verzweifeln, in meinem Reviere schütze ich jeden vor seinen wilden Thieren. Und das ist das Erste, was ich euch anbiete: Sicherheit!

Das Zweite aber ist: mein kleiner Finger. Und habt ihr den erst, so nehmt nur noch die ganze Hand, wohlan! und das Herz dazu! Willkommen hier, willkommen, meine Gastfreunde!"

Also sprach Zarathustra und lachte vor Liebe und Bosheit. Nach dieser Begrüssung verneigten sich seine Gäste abermals und schwiegen ehrfürchtig; der König zur Rechten aber antwortete ihm in ihrem Namen.

"Daran, O Zarathustra, wie du uns Hand und Gruss botest, erkennen wir dich als Zarathustra. Du erniedrigtest dich vor uns; fast thatest du unserer Ehrfurcht wehe –:

– wer aber vermochte gleich dir sich mit solchem Stolze zu erniedrigen? Das richtet uns selber auf, ein Labsal ist es unsern Augen und Herzen.

Dies allein nur zu schaun, stiegen gern wir auf höhere Berge, als dieser Berg ist. Als Schaulustige nämlich kamen wir, wir wollten sehn, was trübe Augen hell macht.

Und siehe, schon ist es vorbei mit allem unsern Nothschrein. Schon steht Sinn und Herz uns offen und ist entzückt. Wenig fehlt: und unser Muth wird muthwillig.

Nichts, O Zarathustra, wächst Erfreulicheres auf Erden, als ein hoher starker Wille: der ist ihr schönstes Gewächs. Eine ganze Landschaft erquickt sich an Einem solchen Baume.

Die Begrüssung

Der Pinie vergleiche ich, wer gleich dir, O Zarathustra, aufwächst: lang, schweigend, hart, allein, besten biegsamsten Holzes, herrlich, –
– zuletzt aber hinausgreifend mit starken grünen Ästen nach seiner Herrschaft, starke Fragen fragend vor Winden und Wettern und was immer auf Höhen heimisch ist,
– stärker antwortend, ein Befehlender, ein Siegreicher: oh wer sollte nicht, solche Gewächse zu schaun, auf hohe Berge steigen?

Deines Baumes hier, O Zarathustra, erlabt sich auch der Düstere, der Mißrathene, an deinem Anblicke wird auch der Unstäte sicher und heilt sein Herz.

Und wahrlich, zu deinem Berge und Baume richten sich heute viele Augen; eine grosse Sehnsucht hat sich aufgemacht, und Manche lernten fragen: wer ist Zarathustra?

Und wem du jemals dein Lied und deinen Honig in's Ohr geträufelt: alle die Versteckten, die Einsiedler, die Zweisiedler sprachen mit Einem Male zu ihrem Herzen:

'Lebt Zarathustra noch? Es lohnt sich nicht mehr zu leben, Alles ist gleich, Alles ist umsonst: oder – wir müssen mit Zarathustra leben!'

'Warum kommt er nicht, der sich so lange ankündigte? also fragen Viele; verschlang ihn die Einsamkeit? Oder sollen wir wohl zu ihm kommen?'

Nun geschieht's, daß die Einsamkeit selber mürbe wird und zerbricht, einem Grabe gleich, das zerbricht und seine Todten nicht mehr halten kann. Überall sieht man Auferstandene.

Nun steigen und steigen die Wellen um deinen Berg, O Zarathustra. Und wie hoch auch deine Höhe ist, Viele müssen zu dir hinauf; dein Nachen soll nicht lange mehr im Trocknen sitzen.

Und daß wir Verzweifelnde jetzt in deine Höhle kamen und schon nicht mehr verzweifeln: ein Wahr- und Vorzeichen ist es nur, davon, daß Bessere zu dir unterwegs sind, –

– denn er selber ist zu dir unterwegs, der letzte Rest Gottes unter Menschen, das ist: alle die Menschen der grossen Sehnsucht, des grossen Ekels, des grossen Überdrusses,

– Alle, die nicht leben wollen, oder sie lernen wieder hoffen – oder sie lernen von dir, O Zarathustra, die grosse Hoffnung!"

Also sprach der König zur Rechten und ergriff die Hand Zarathustras, um sie zu küssen; aber Zarathustra wehrte seiner Verehrung und trat erschreckt zurück, schweigend und plötzlich wie in weite Fernen

entfliehend. Nach einer kleinen Weile aber war er schon wieder bei seinen Gästen, blickte sie mit hellen, prüfenden Augen an und sprach:
Meine Gäste, ihr höheren Menschen, ich will deutsch und deutlich mit euch reden. Nicht auf euch wartete ich hier in diesen Bergen.
("Deutsch und deutlich? Daß Gott erbarm! sagte hier der König zur Linken, bei Seite; man merkt, er kennt die lieben Deutschen nicht, dieser Weise aus dem Morgenlande!
Aber er meint 'deutsch und derb' – wohlan! Das ist heutzutage noch nicht der schlimmste Geschmack!")
"Ihr mögt wahrlich insgesammt höhere Menschen sein, fuhr Zarathustra fort: aber für mich – seid ihr nicht hoch und stark genug.
Für mich, das heißt: für das Unerbittliche, das in mir schweigt, aber nicht immer schweigen wird. Und gehört ihr zu mir, so doch nicht als mein rechter Arm.
Wer nämlich selber auf kranken und zarten Beinen steht, gleich euch, der will vor Allem, ob er's weiss oder sich verbirgt: daß er geschont werde.
Meine Arme und meine Beine aber schone ich nicht, ich schone meine Krieger nicht: wieso könntet ihr zu meinem Kriege taugen?
Mit euch verdürbe ich mir jeden Sieg noch. Und Mancher von euch fiele schon um, wenn er nur den lauten Schall meiner Trommeln hörte.
Auch seid ihr mir nicht schön genug und wohlgeboren. Ich brauche reine glatte Spiegel für meine Lehren; auf eurer Oberfläche verzerrt sich noch mein eignes Bildniss.
Eure Schultern drückt manche Last, manche Erinnerung; manch schlimmer Zwerg hockt in euren Winkeln. Es giebt verborgenen Pöbel auch in euch.
Und seid ihr auch hoch und höherer Art: Vieles an euch ist krumm und mißgestalt. Da ist kein Schmied in der Welt, der euch mir zurecht und gerade schlüge.
Ihr seid nur Brücken: mögen Höhere auf euch hinüber schreiten! Ihr bedeutet Stufen: so zürnt Dem nicht, der über euch hinweg in seine Höhe steigt!
Aus eurem Samen mag auch mir einst ein echter Sohn und vollkommener Erbe wachsen: aber das ist ferne. Ihr selber seid Die nicht, welchen mein Erbgut und Name zugehört.
Nicht auf euch warte ich hier in diesen Bergen, nicht mit euch darf ich zum letzten Male niedersteigen. Als Vorzeichen kamt ihr mir nur, daß schon Höhere zu mir unterwegs sind, –

Die Begrüssung

– nicht die Menschen der grossen Sehnsucht, des grossen Ekels, des grossen Überdrusses und Das, was ihr den Überrest Gottes nanntet.
– Nein! Nein! Dreimal Nein! Auf Andere warte ich hier in diesen Bergen und will meinen Fuss nicht ohne sie von dannen heben,
– auf Höhere, Stärkere, Sieghaftere, Wohlgemuthere, Solche, die rechtwinklig gebaut sind an Leib und Seele: lachende Löwen müssen kommen!

O, meine Gastfreunde, ihr Wunderlichen, – hörtet ihr noch Nichts von meinen Kindern? Und dass sie zu mir unterwegs sind?

Sprecht mir doch von meinen Gärten, von meinen glückseligen Inseln, von meiner neuen schönen Art, – warum sprecht ihr mir nicht davon?

Dies Gastgeschenk erbitte ich mir von eurer Liebe, dass ihr mir von meinen Kindern sprecht. Hierzu bin ich reich, hierzu ward ich arm: was gab ich nicht hin,
– was gäbe ich nicht hin, dass ich Eins hätte: diese Kinder, diese lebendige Pflanzung, diese Lebensbäume meines Willens und meiner höchsten Hoffnung!"

Also sprach Zarathustra und hielt plötzlich inne in seiner Rede: denn ihn überfiel seine Sehnsucht, und er schloss Augen und Mund vor der Bewegung seines Herzens. Und auch alle seine Gäste schwiegen und standen still und bestürzt: nur dass der alte Wahrsager mit Händen und Gebärden Zeichen gab.

Das Abendmahl

An dieser Stelle nämlich unterbrach der Wahrsager die Begrüssung Zarathustras und seiner Gäste: er drängte sich vor, wie Einer, der keine Zeit zu verlieren hat, faßte die Hand Zarathustras und rief: "Aber Zarathustra!

Eins ist nothwendiger als das Andre, so redest du selber: wohlan, Eins ist mir jetzt nothwendiger als alles Andere.

Ein Wort zur rechten Zeit: hast du mich nicht zum Mahle eingeladen? Und hier sind viele, die lange Wege machten. Du willst uns doch nicht mit Reden abspeisen?

Auch gedachtet ihr Alle mir schon zu viel des Erfrierens, Ertrinkens, Erstickens und andrer Leibes-Nothstände. Keiner aber gedachte meines Nothstandes, nämlich des Verhungerns -"

(Also sprach der Wahrsager; wie die Thiere Zarathustras aber diese Worte hörten, liefen sie vor Schrecken davon. Denn sie sahen, daß was sie auch am Tage heimgebracht hatten, nicht genug sein werde, den Einen Wahrsager zu stopfen.)

"Eingerechnet das Verdursten, fuhr der Wahrsager fort. Und ob ich schon Wasser hier plätschern höre, gleich Reden der Weisheit, nämlich reichlich und unermüdlich: ich - will Wein!

Nicht jeder ist gleich Zarathustra ein geborner Wassertrinker. Wasser taugt auch nicht für Müde und Verwelkte: uns gebührt Wein, - der erst giebt plötzliches Genesen und stegreife Gesundheit!"

Bei dieser Gelegenheit, da der Wahrsager nach Wein begehrte, geschah es, daß auch der König zur Linken, der Schweigsame, einmal zu Worte kam. "Für Wein, sprach er, trugen wir Sorge, ich sammt meinem Bruder, dem Könige zur Rechten: wir haben Weins genug, - einen ganzen Esel voll. So fehlt Nichts als Brot."

"Brot! entgegnete Zarathustra und lachte dazu. Nur gerade Brot haben Einsiedler nicht. Aber der Mensch lebt nicht vom Brot allein, sondern auch vom Fleische guter Lämmer, deren ich zwei habe:

- Die soll man geschwinde schlachten und würzig, mit Salbei, zubereiten: so liebe ich's. Und auch an Wurzeln und Früchten fehlt es nicht, gut genug selbst für Lecker- und Schmeckerlinge; noch an Nüssen und andern Räthseln zum Knacken.

Das Abendmahl

Also wollen wir in Kürze eine gute Mahlzeit machen. Wer aber mit essen will, muss auch mit Hand anlegen, auch die Könige. Bei Zarathustra nämlich darf auch ein König Koch sein."

Mit diesem Vorschlage war Allen nach dem Herzen geredet: nur daß der freiwillige Bettler sich gegen Fleisch und Wein und Würzen sträubte.

"Nun hört mir doch diesen Schlemmer Zarathustra! sagte er scherzhaft: geht man dazu in Höhlen und Hoch-Gebirge, daß man solche Mahlzeiten macht? Nun freilich verstehe ich, was er einst uns lehrte: 'Gelobt sei die kleine Armuth!' Und warum er die Bettler abschaffen will."

"Sei guter Dinge, antwortete ihm Zarathustra, wie ich es bin. Bleibe bei deiner Sitte, du Trefflicher, malme deine Körner, trink dein Wasser, lobe deine Küche: wenn sie dich nur fröhlich macht!

Ich bin ein Gesetz nur für die Meinen, ich bin kein Gesetz für Alle. Wer aber zu mir gehört, der muss von starken Knochen sein, auch von leichten Füssen, –

– lustig zu Kriegen und Festen, kein Düsterling, kein Traum-Hans, bereit zum Schwersten wie zu seinem Feste, gesund und heil.

Das Beste gehört den Meinen und mir; und giebt man's uns nicht, so nehmen wir's: – die beste Nahrung, den reinsten Himmel, die stärksten Gedanken, die schönsten Fraun!" –

Also sprach Zarathustra; der König zur Rechten aber entgegnete: "Seltsam! Vernahm man je solche kluge Dinge aus dem Munde eines Weisen?

Und wahrlich, das ist das Seltsamste an einem Weisen, wenn er zu alledem auch noch klug und kein Esel ist."

Also sprach der König zur Rechten und wunderte sich; der Esel aber sagte zu seiner Rede mit bösem Willen J-A. Dies aber war der Anfang von jener langen Mahlzeit, welche "das Abendmahl" in den Historien-Büchern genannt wird. Bei derselben aber wurde von nichts Anderem geredet als *vom höheren Menschen.*

Vom höheren Menschen

1.

Als ich zum ersten Male zu den Menschen kam, da that ich die Einsiedler-Thorheit, die grosse Thorheit: ich stellte mich auf den Markt.

Und als ich zu Allen redete, redete ich zu Keinem. Des Abends aber waren Seiltänzer meine Genossen, und Leichname; und ich selber fast ein Leichnam.

Mit dem neuen Morgen aber kam mir eine neue Wahrheit: da lernte ich sprechen "Was geht mich Markt und Pöbel und Pöbel-Lärm und lange Pöbel-Ohren an!"

Ihr höheren Menschen, Dies lernt von mir: auf dem Markt glaubt Niemand an höhere Menschen. Und wollt ihr dort reden, wohlan! Der Pöbel aber blinzelt "wir sind Alle gleich."

"Ihr höheren Menschen, – so blinzelt der Pöbel – es giebt keine höheren Menschen, wir sind Alle gleich, Mensch ist Mensch, vor Gott – sind wir Alle gleich!"

Vor Gott! – Nun aber starb dieser Gott. Vor dem Pöbel aber wollen wir nicht gleich sein. Ihr höheren Menschen, geht weg vom Markt!

2.

Vor Gott! – Nun aber starb dieser Gott! Ihr höheren Menschen, dieser Gott war eure grösste Gefahr.

Seit er im Grabe liegt, seid ihr erst wieder auferstanden. Nun erst kommt der grosse Mittag, nun erst wird der höhere Mensch – Herr!

Verstandet ihr dies Wort, O meine Brüder? Ihr seid erschreckt: wird euren Herzen schwindlig? Klafft euch hier der Abgrund? Klafft euch hier der Höllenhund?

Wohlan! Wohlauf! Ihr höheren Menschen! Nun erst kreißt der Berg der Menschen-Zukunft. Gott starb: nun wollen wir, – daß der Übermensch lebe.

3.

Die Sorglichsten fragen heute: "wie bleibt der Mensch erhalten?" Zarathustra aber fragt als der Einzige und Erste: "wie wird der Mensch überwunden?"

Der Übermensch liegt mir am Herzen, der ist mein Erstes und Einziges, – und nicht der Mensch: nicht der Nächste, nicht der Ärmste, nicht der Leidendste, nicht der Beste –

O meine Brüder, was ich lieben kann am Menschen, das ist, dass er ein Übergang ist und ein Untergang. Und auch an euch ist vieles, das mich lieben und hoffen macht.

Dass ihr verachtetet, ihr höheren Menschen, das macht mich hoffen. Die grossen Verachtenden nämlich sind die grossen Verehrenden.

Dass ihr verzweifeltet, daran ist Viel zu ehren. Denn ihr lerntet nicht, wie ihr euch ergäbet, ihr lerntet die kleinen Klugheiten nicht.

Heute nämlich wurden die kleinen Leute Herr: die predigen Alle Ergebung und Bescheidung und Klugheit und Fleiss und Rücksicht und das lange Und-so-weiter der kleinen Tugenden.

Was von Weibsart ist, was von Knechtsart stammt und sonderlich der Pöbel-Mischmasch: Das will nun Herr werden alles Menschen-Schicksals – oh Ekel! Ekel! Ekel!

Das frägt und frägt und wird nicht müde: "Wie erhält sich der Mensch, am besten, am längsten, am angenehmsten?" Damit – sind sie die Herrn von heute.

Diese Herrn von heute überwindet mir, o meine Brüder, – diese kleinen Leute: die sind des Übermenschen grösste Gefahr!

Überwindet mir, ihr höheren Menschen, die kleinen Tugenden, die kleinen Klugheiten, die Sandkorn-Rücksichten, den Ameisen-Kribbelkram, das erbärmliche Behagen, das "Glück der Meisten" –!

Und lieber verzweifelt, als dass ihr euch ergebt. Und, wahrlich, ich liebe euch dafür, dass ihr heute nicht zu leben wisst, ihr höheren Menschen! So nämlich lebt ihr – am Besten!

4.

Habt ihr Muth, o meine Brüder? Seid ihr herzhaft? Nicht Muth vor Zeugen, sondern Einsiedler- und Adler-Muth, dem auch kein Gott mehr zusieht?

Kalte Seelen, Maulthiere, Blinde, Trunkene heissen mir nicht herzhaft. Herz hat, wer Furcht kennt, aber Furcht zwingt, er den Abgrund sieht, aber mit Stolz.

Wer den Abgrund sieht, aber mit Adlers-Augen, wer mit Adlers-Krallen den Abgrund fasst: der hat Muth. — —

5.

"Der Mensch ist böse" — so sprachen mir zum Troste alle Weisesten. Ach, wenn es heute nur noch wahr ist! Denn das Böse ist des Menschen beste Kraft."

Der Mensch muss besser und böser werden" — so lehre ich. Das Böseste ist nöthig zu des Übermenschen Bestem.

Das mochte gut sein für jenen Prediger der kleinen Leute, daß er litt und trug an des Menschen Sünde. Ich aber erfreue mich der grossen Sünde als meines grossen Trostes. —

Solches ist aber nicht für lange Ohren gesagt. Jedwedes Wort gehört auch nicht in jedes Maul. Das sind feine ferne Dinge: nach denen sollen nicht Schafs-Klauen greifen!

6.

Ihr höheren Menschen, meint ihr, ich sei da, gut zu machen, was ihr schlecht machtet?

Oder ich wollte fürderhin auch Leidende bequemer betten? Oder auch Unstäten, Verirrten, Verkletterten neue leichtere Fußsteige zeigen?

Nein! Nein! Dreimal Nein! Immer Mehr, immer Bessere eurer Art sollen zu Grunde gehn, — denn ihr sollt es immer schlimmer und härter haben. So allein —

– so allein wächst der Mensch in die Höhe, wo der Blitz ihn trifft und zerbricht: hoch genug für den Blitz!

Auf Weniges, auf Langes, auf Fernes geht mein Sinn und meine Sehnsucht: was gienge mich euer kleines, vieles, kurzes Elend an!

Ihr leidet mir noch nicht genug! Denn ihr leidet an euch, ihr littet noch nicht am Menschen. Ihr würdet lügen, wenn ihr's anders sagtet! Ihr leidet Alle nicht, woran ich litt. – –

7.

Es ist mir nicht genug, dass der Blitz nicht mehr schadet. Nicht ableiten will ich ihn: er soll lernen für mich – arbeiten. –

Meine Weisheit sammelt sich lange schon gleich einer Wolke, sie wird stiller und dunkler. So thut jede Weisheit, welche einst Blitze gebären soll. –

Diesen Menschen von Heute will ich nicht Licht sein, nicht Licht heissen. Die – will ich blenden: Blitz meiner Weisheit! Stich ihnen die Augen aus!

8.

Wollt Nichts über euer Vermögen: es giebt eine schlimme Falschheit bei Solchen, die über ihr Vermögen wollen.

Sonderlich, wenn sie grosse Dinge wollen! Denn sie wecken Misstrauen gegen grosse Dinge, diese feinen Falschmünzer und Schauspieler: –

– bis sie endlich falsch vor sich selber sind, schieläugig, übertünchter Wurmfrass, bemäntelt durch starke Worte, durch Aushänge-Tugenden, durch glänzende falsche Werke.

Habt da eine gute Vorsicht, ihr höheren Menschen! Nichts nämlich gilt mir heute kostbarer und seltner als Redlichkeit.

Ist dies Heute nicht des Pöbels? Pöbel aber weiss nicht, was gross, was klein, was gerade und redlich ist: der ist unschuldig krumm, der lügt immer.

9.

Habt heute ein gutes Misstrauen, ihr höheren Menschen, ihr Beherzten! Ihr Offenherzigen! Und haltet eure Gründe geheim! Dies Heute nämlich ist des Pöbels.

Was der Pöbel ohne Gründe einst glauben lernte, wer könnte ihm durch Gründe Das – umwerfen?

Und auf dem Markte überzeugt man mit Gebärden. Aber Gründe machen den Pöbel misstrauisch.

Und wenn da einmal Wahrheit zum Siege kam, so fragt euch mit gutem Misstrauen: "welch starker Irrthum hat für sie gekämpft!"

Hütet euch auch vor den Gelehrten! Die hassen euch: denn sie sind unfruchtbar! Sie haben kalte vertrocknete Augen, vor ihnen liegt jeder Vogel entfedert.

Solche brüsten sich damit, dass sie nicht lügen: aber Ohnmacht zur Lüge ist lange noch nicht Liebe zur Wahrheit. Hütet euch!

Freiheit von Fieber ist lange noch nicht Erkenntnis! Ausgekälteten Geistern glaube ich nicht. Wer nicht lügen kann, weiss nicht, was Wahrheit ist.

10.

Wollt ihr hoch hinaus, so braucht die eignen Beine! Lasst euch nicht empor tragen, setzt euch nicht auf fremde Rükken und Köpfe!

Du aber stiegst zu Pferde? Du reitest nun hurtig hinauf zu deinem Ziele? Wohlan, mein Freund! Aber dein lahmer Fuss sitzt auch mit zu Pferde!

Wenn du an deinem Ziele bist, wenn du von deinem Pferde springst: auf deiner Höhe gerade, du höherer Mensch – wirst du stolpern!

11.

Ihr Schaffenden, ihr höheren Menschen! Man ist nur für das eigne Kind schwanger.

Lasst euch Nichts vorreden, einreden! Wer ist denn euer Nächster? Und handelt ihr auch "für den Nächsten", – ihr schafft doch nicht für ihn!

Verlernt mir doch dies "für", ihr Schaffenden: eure Tugend gerade will es, dass ihr kein Ding mit "für" und "um" und "weil" thut. Gegen diese falschen kleinen Worte sollt ihr euer Ohr zukleben.

Das "für den Nächsten" ist die Tugend nur der kleinen Leute: da heißt es "gleich und gleich" und "Hand wäscht Hand": – sie haben nicht Recht noch Kraft zu eurem Eigennutz!

In eurem Eigennutz, ihr Schaffenden, ist der Schwangeren Vorsicht und Vorsehung! Was Niemand noch mit Augen sah, die Frucht: die schirmt und schont und nährt eure ganze Liebe.

Wo eure ganze Liebe ist, bei eurem Kinde, da ist auch eure ganze Tugend! Euer Werk, euer Wille ist euer "Nächster": lasst euch keine falschen Werthe einreden!

12.

Ihr Schaffenden, ihr höheren Menschen! Wer gebären muss, der ist krank; wer aber geboren hat, ist unrein.

Fragt die Weiber: man gebiert nicht, weil es Vergnügen macht. Der Schmerz macht Hühner und Dichter gackern.

Ihr Schaffenden, an euch ist viel Unreines. Das macht, ihr musstet Mütter sein.

Ein neues Kind: oh wie viel neuer Schmutz kam auch zur Welt! Geht bei Seite! Und wer geboren hat, soll seine Seele rein waschen!

13.

Seid nicht tugendhaft über eure Kräfte! Und wollt Nichts von euch wider die Wahrscheinlichkeit!

Geht in den Fusstapfen, wo schon eurer Väter Tugend gierig! Wie wolltet ihr hoch steigen, wenn nicht eurer Väter Wille mit euch steigt?

Wer aber Erstling sein will, sehe zu, daß er nicht auch Letzling werde! Und wo die Laster eurer Väter sind, darin sollt ihr nicht Heilige bedeuten wollen!

Wessen Väter es mit Weibern hielten und mit starken Weinen und Wildschweinen: was wäre es, wenn Der von sich Keuschheit wollte?

Eine Narrheit wäre es! Viel, wahrlich, dünkt es mich für einen Solchen, wenn er Eines oder zweier oder dreier Weiber Mann ist.

Und stiftete er Klöster und schriebe über die Thür: "der Weg zum Heiligen," – ich spräche doch: wozu! es ist eine neue Narrheit!

Er stiftete sich selber ein Zucht- und Fluchthaus: wohl bekomm's! Aber ich glaube nicht daran.

In der Einsamkeit wächst, was Einer in sie bringt, auch das innere Vieh. Solchergestalt widerräth sich Vielen die Einsamkeit.

Gab es Schmutzigeres bisher auf Erden als Wüsten-Heilige? Um die herum war nicht nur der Teufel los, – sondern auch das Schwein.

14.

Scheu, beschämt, ungeschickt, einem Tiger gleich, dem der Sprung mißrieth: also, ihr höheren Menschen, sah ich oft euch bei Seite schleichen. Ein Wurf mißrieth euch.

Aber, ihr Würfelspieler, was liegt daran! Ihr lerntet nicht spielen und spotten, wie man spielen und spotten muss! Sitzen wir nicht immer an einem grossen Spott- und Spieltische?

Und wenn auch Grosses mißrieth, seid ihr selber darum – mißrathen? Und mißriethet ihr selber, mißrieth darum – der Mensch? Mißrieth aber der Mensch: wohlan! wohlauf!

15.

Je höher von Art, je seltener geräth ein Ding. Ihr höheren Menschen hier, seid ihr nicht alle – mißgerathen?

Seid guten Muths, was liegt daran! Wie Vieles ist noch möglich! Lernt über euch selber lachen, wie man lachen muss!

Was Wunders auch, daß ihr mißriethet und halb gerathet, ihr Halb-Zerbrochenen! Drängt und stösst sich nicht in euch – des Menschen Zukunft?

Des Menschen Fernstes, Tiefstes, Sternen-Höchstes, seine ungeheure Kraft: schäumt Das nicht alles gegen einander in eurem Topfe?

Was Wunders, daß mancher Topf zerbricht! Lernt über euch lachen, wie man lachen muss! Ihr höheren Menschen, oh wie Vieles ist noch möglich!

Und wahrlich, wie Viel gerieth schon! Wie reich ist diese Erde an kleinen guten vollkommenen Dingen, an Wohlgerathenem!

Stellt kleine gute vollkommne Dinge um euch, ihr höheren Menschen! Deren goldene Reife heilt das Herz. Vollkommnes lehrt hoffen.

16.

Welches war hier auf Erden bisher die grösste Sünde? War es nicht das Wort Dessen, der sprach: "Wehe Denen, die hier lachen!"

Fand er zum Lachen auf der Erde selber keine Gründe? So suchte er nur schlecht. Ein Kind findet hier noch Gründe.

Der – liebte nicht genug: sonst hätte er auch uns geliebt, die Lachenden! Aber er hasste und höhnte uns, Heulen und Zähneklappern verhiess er uns.

Muss man denn gleich fluchen, wo man nicht liebt? Das – dünkt mich ein schlechter Geschmack. Aber so that er, dieser Unbedingte. Er kam vom Pöbel.

Und er selber liebte nur nicht genug: sonst hätte er weniger gezürnt, daß man ihn nicht liebe. Alle grosse Liebe *will* nicht Liebe: – die will mehr.

Geht aus dem Wege allen solchen Unbedingten! Das ist eine arme kranke Art, eine Pöbel-Art: sie sehn schlimm diesem Leben zu, sie haben den bösen Blick für diese Erde.

Geht aus dem Wege allen solchen Unbedingten! Sie haben Schwere Füsse und schwüle Herzen: – sie *wissen* nicht zu tanzen. Wie möchte Solchen wohl die Erde leicht sein!

17.

Krumm kommen alle guten Dinge ihrem Ziele nahe. Gleich Katzen machen sie Buckel, sie schnurren innewendig vor ihrem nahen Glücke, – alle guten Dinge lachen.

Der Schritt verräth, ob Einer schon auf seiner Bahn schreitet: so seht mich gehn! Wer aber seinem Ziel nahe kommt, der tanzt.

Und, wahrlich, zum Standbild ward ich nicht, noch stehe ich nicht da, starr, stumpf, steinern, eine Säule; ich liebe geschwindes Laufen.

Und wenn es auf Erden auch Moor und dicke Trübsal giebt: wer leichte Füsse hat, läuft über Schlamm noch hinweg und tanzt wie auf gefegtem Eise.

Erhebt eure Herzen, meine Brüder, hoch! höher! Und vergesst mir auch die Beine nicht! Erhebt auch eure Beine, ihr guten Tänzer, und besser noch: ihr steht auch auf dem Kopf!

18.

Diese Krone des Lachenden, diese Rosenkranz-Krone: ich selber setzte mir diese Krone auf, ich selber sprach heilig mein Gelächter. Keinen Anderen fand ich heute stark genug dazu.

Zarathustra der Tänzer, Zarathustra der Leichte, der mit den Flügeln winkt, ein Flugbereiter, allen Vögeln zuwinkend, bereit und fertig, ein Selig-Leichtfertiger: -

Zarathustra der Wahrsager, Zarathustra der Wahrlacher, kein Ungeduldiger, kein Unbedingter, Einer, der Sprünge und Seitensprünge liebt; ich selber setzte mir diese Krone auf!

19.

Erhebt eure Herzen, meine Brüder, hoch! höher! Und vergesst mir auch die Beine nicht! Erhebt auch eure Beine, ihr guten Tänzer, und besser noch: ihr steht auch auf dem Kopf!

Es giebt auch im Glück schweres Gethier, es giebt Plumpfüssler von Anbeginn. Wunderlich müht sie sich ab, einem Elephanten gleich, der sich müht auf dem Kopf zu stehn.

Besser aber noch närrisch sein vor Glücke als närrisch vor Unglücke, besser plump tanzen als lahm gehn. So lernt mir doch meine Weisheit ab: auch das schlimmste Ding hat zwei gute Kehrseiten, -

- auch das schlimmste Ding hat gute Tanzbeine: so lernt mir doch auch selbst, ihr höheren Menschen, auf eure rechten Beine stellen!

So verlernt mir doch Trübsal-Blasen und alle Pöbel-Traurigkeit! Oh wie traurig dünken mich heute des Pöbels Hanswürste noch! Dies Heute aber ist des Pöbels.

20.

Dem Winde thut mir gleich, wann er aus seinen Berghöhlen stürzt: nach seiner eignen Pfeife will er tanzen, die Meere zittern und hüpfen unter seinen Fusstapfen.

Der den Eseln Flügel giebt, der Löwinnen melkt, gelobt sei dieser gute unbändige Geist, der allem Heute und allem Pöbel wie ein Sturmwind kommt, -

– der Distel- und Tiftelköpfen feind ist und allen welken Blättern und Unkräutern: gelobt sei dieser wilde gute freie Sturmgeist, welcher auf Mooren und Trübsalen wie auf Wiesen tanzt!

Der die Pöbel-Schwindhunde hasst und alles mißrathene düstere Gezücht: gelobt sei dieser Geist aller freien Geister, der lachende Sturm, welcher allen Schwarzsichtigen, Schwärsüchtigen Staub in die Augen bläst!

Ihr höheren Menschen, euer Schlimmstes ist: ihr lerntet alle nicht tanzen, wie man tanzen muss – über euch hinweg tanzen! Was liegt daran, daß ihr mißriethet!

Wie Vieles ist noch möglich! So lernt doch über euch hinweg lachen! Erhebt eure Herzen, ihr guten Tänzer, hoch! höher! Und vergesst mir auch das gute Lachen nicht!

Diese Krone des Lachenden, diese Rosenkranz-Krone: euch, meinen Brüdern, werfe ich diese Krone zu! Das Lachen sprach ich heilig; ihr höheren Menschen, lernt mir – lachen!

Das Lied der Schwermuth

1.

Als Zarathustra diese Reden sprach, stand er nahe dem Eingange seiner Höhle; mit den letzten Worten aber entschlüpfte er seinen Gästen und floh für eine kurze Weile in's Freie.
"Oh reine Gerüche um mich, rief er aus, oh selige Stille um mich! Aber wo sind meine Thiere? Heran, heran, mein Adler und meine Schlange!
Sagt mir doch, meine Thiere: diese höheren Menschen insgesammt – riechen sie vielleicht nicht gut? Oh reine Gerüche um mich! Jetzo weiss und fühle ich erst, wie ich auch, meine Thiere, liebe."
– Und Zarathustra sprach nochmals: "ich liebe euch, meine Thiere!" Der Adler aber und die Schlange drängten sich an ihn, als er diese Worte sprach, und sahen zu ihm hinauf. Solchergestalt waren sie zu drei still beisammen und schnüffelten und schlürften mit einander die gute Luft. Denn die Luft war hier draussen besser als bei den höheren Menschen.

2.

Kaum aber hatte Zarathustra seine Höhle verlassen, da erhob sich der alte Zauberer, sah listig umher und sprach: "Er ist hinaus!
Und schon, ihr höheren Menschen – daß ich euch mit diesem Lob- und Schmeichel-Namen kitzle, gleich ihm selber – schon fällt mich mein schlimmer Trug- und Zaubergeist an, mein schwermüthiger Teufel,
– welcher diesem Zarathustra ein Widersacher ist aus dem Grunde: vergebt es ihm! Nun will er vor euch zaubern, er hat gerade seine Stunde; umsonst ringe ich mit diesem bösen Geiste.
Euch Allen, welche Ehren ihr auch mit Worten geben mögt, ob ihr euch 'die freien Geister' nennt oder 'die Wahrhaftigen' oder 'die Büsser des Geistes' oder 'die Entfesselten' oder 'die grossen Sehnsüchtigen' –
– euch Allen, die ihr am grossen Ekel leidet gleich mir, denen der alte Gott starb und noch kein neuer Gott in Wiegen und Windeln liegt, – euch Allen ist mein böser Geist und Zauber-Teufel hold.
Ich kenne euch, ihr höheren Menschen, ich kenne ihn, – ich kenne auch diesen Unhold, den ich wider Willen liebe, diesen Zarathustra: er selber dünkt mich öfter gleich einer schönen Heiligen-Larve,

– gleich einem neuen wunderlichen Mummenschanze, in dem sich mein böser Geist, der schwermüthige Teufel, gefällt: – ich liebe Zarathustra, so dünkt mich oft, um meines bösen Geistes Willen. –
Aber schon fällt der mich an und zwingt mich, dieser Geist der Schwermuth, dieser Abend-Dämmerungs-Teufel: und, wahrlich, ihr höheren Menschen, es gelüstet ihn –
– macht nur die Augen auf! – es gelüstet ihn, nackt zu kommen, ob männlich, ob weiblich, noch weiss ich's nicht: aber er kommt, er zwingt mich, wehe! macht eure Sinne auf!
Der Tag klingt ab, allen Dingen kommt nun der Abend, auch den besten Dingen; hört nun und seht, ihr höheren Menschen, welcher Teufel, ob Mann, ob Weib, dieser Geist der Abend-Schwermuth ist!"
Also sprach der alte Zauberer, sah listig umher und griff dann zu seiner Harfe.

3.

Bei abgehellter Luft,
Wenn schon des Thaus Tröstung
Zur Erde niederquillt,
Unsichtbar, auch ungehört: –
Denn zartes Schuhwerk trägt
Der Tröster Thau gleich allen Trost-Milden –:
Gedenkst du da, gedenkst du, heisses Herz,
Wie einst du durstetest,
Nach himmlischen Thränen und Thau-Geträufel
Versengt und müde durstetest,
Dieweil auf gelben Gras-Pfaden
Boshaft abendliche Sonnenblicke
Durch schwarze Bäume um dich liefen,
Blendende Sonnen-Gluthblicke, schadenfrohe?

"Der Wahrheit Freier? Du! – so höhnten sie –
Nein! Nur ein Dichter!
Ein Thier, ein listiges, raubendes, schleichendes,
Das lügen muss,
Das wissentlich, willentlich lügen muss:
Nach Beute lüstern,
Bunt verlarvt,

Sich selber Larve,
Sich selbst zur Beute –
Das – der Wahrheit Freier?
Nein! Nur Narr! Nur Dichter!
Nur Buntes redend,
Aus Narren-Larven bunt herausschreiend,
Herumsteigend auf lügnerischen Wort-Brücken,
Auf bunten Regenbogen,
Zwischen falschen Himmeln
Und falschen Erden,
Herumschweifend, herumschwebend, –
Nur Narr! Nur Dichter!

Das – der Wahrheit Freier?
Nicht still, starr, glatt, kalt,
Zum Bilde worden,
Zur Gottes-Säule,
Nicht aufgestellt vor Tempeln,
Eines Gottes Thürwart:
Nein! feindselig solchen Wahrheits-Standbildern,
In jeder Wildniss heimischer als vor Tempeln,
Voll Katzen-Muthwillens,
Durch jedes Fenster springend
Husch! in jeden Zufall,
Jedem Urwalde zuschnüffelnd,
Süchtig-sehnsüchtig zuschnüffelnd,
Daß du in Urwäldern
Unter buntgefleckten Raubthieren
Sündlich-gesund und bunt und schön liefest,
Mit lüsternen Lefzen,
Selig-höhnisch, selig-höllisch, selig-blutgierig,
Raubend, schleichend, lügend liefest: –

Oder, dem Adler gleich, der lange,
Lange starr in Abgründe blickt,
In seine Abgründe: – –
Oh wie sie sich hier hinab,
Hinunter, hinein,
In immer tiefere Tiefen ringeln! –

Dann,
plötzlich, geraden Zugs,
Gezückten Flugs,
Auf Lämmer stossen,
Jach hinab, heisshungrig,
Nach Lämmern lüstern,
Gram allen Lamms-Seelen,
Grimmig-gram Allem, was blickt
Schafmässig, lammäugig, krauswollig,
Grau, mit Lamms-Schafs-Wohlwollen!

Also
Adlerhaft, pantherhaft
Sind des Dichters Sehnsüchte,
Sind deine Sehnsüchte unter tausend Larven,
Du Narr! Du Dichter!

Der du den Menschen schautest
So Gott als Schaf –:
Den Gott zerreissen im Menschen
Wie das Schaf im Menschen,
Und zerreissend lachen –
Das, Das ist deine Seligkeit!
Eines Panthers und Adlers Seligkeit!
Eines Dichters und Narren Seligkeit!" – –

Bei abgehellter Luft,
Wenn schon des Monds Sichel
Grün zwischen Purpurröthen
Und neidisch hinschleicht:
– dem Tage feind,
Mit jedem Schritte heimlich
An Rosen-Hängematten
Hinsichelnd, bis sie sinken,
Nacht-abwärts blass hinabsinken: –

So sank ich selber einstmals
Aus meinem Wahrheits-Wahnsinne,
Aus meinen Tages-Sehnsüchten,
Des Tages müde, krank vom Lichte,
— sank abwärts, abendwärts, schattenwärts:
Von Einer Wahrheit
Verbrannt und durstig:
— gedenkst du noch, gedenkst du, heisses Herz,
Wie da du durstetest?
— Daß ich verbannt sei
Von aller Wahrheit,
Nur Narr!
Nur Dichter!

Von der Wissenschaft

Also sang der Zauberer; und Alle, die beisammen waren, giengen gleich Vögeln unvermerkt in das Netz seiner listigen und schwermüthigen Wollust. Nur der Gewissenhafte des Geistes war nicht eingefangen: er nahm flugs dem Zauberer die Harfe weg und rief "Luft! Lasst gute Luft herein! Lass Zarathustra herein! Du machst diese Höhle schwül und giftig, du schlimmer alter Zauberer!

Du verführst, du Falscher, Feiner, zu unbekannten Begierden und Wildnissen. Und wehe, wenn Solche, wie du, von der Wahrheit Redens und Wesens machen!

Wehe allen freien Geistern, welche nicht vor solchen Zauberern auf der Hut sind! Dahin ist es mit ihrer Freiheit: du lehrst und lockst zurück in Gefängnisse, —

— du alter schwermüthiger Teufel, aus deiner Klage klingt eine Lockpfeife, du gleichst Solchen, welche mit ihrem Lobe der Keuschheit heimlich zu Wollüsten laden!"

Also sprach der Gewissenhafte; der alte Zauberer aber blickte um sich, genoss seines Sieges und verschluckte darüber den Verdruss, welchen ihm der Gewissenhafte machte. "Sei still! sagte er mit bescheidener Stimme, gute Lieder wollen gut wiederhallen; nach guten Liedern soll man lange schweigen.

So thun es diese Alle, die höheren Menschen. Du aber hast wohl Wenig von meinem Lied verstanden? In dir ist Wenig von einem Zaubergeiste."

"Du lobst mich, entgegnete der Gewissenhafte, indem du mich von dir abtrennst, wohlan! Aber ihr Anderen, was sehe ich? Ihr sitzt alle noch mit lüsternen Augen da —:

Ihr freien Seelen, wohin ist eure Freiheit! Fast, dünkt mich's, gleicht ihr Solchen, die lange schlimmen tanzenden nackten Mädchen zusahn: eure Seelen tanzen selber!

In euch, ihr höheren Menschen, muss Mehr von Dem sein, was der Zauberer seinen bösen Zauber- und Truggeist nennt: — wir müssen wohl verschieden sein.

Und wahrlich, wir sprachen und dachten genug mitsammen, ehe Zarathustra heimkam zu seiner Höhle, als daß ich nicht wüsste: wir sind verschieden.

Wir suchen Verschiednes auch hier oben, ihr und ich. Ich nämlich suche mehr Sicherheit, desshalb kam ich zu Zarathustra. Der nämlich ist noch der festeste Thurm und Wille –

– heute, wo Alles wackelt, wo alle Erde bebt. Ihr aber, wenn ich eure Augen sehe, die ihr macht, fast dünkt mich's, ihr sucht mehr Unsicherheit,

– mehr Schauder, mehr Gefahr, mehr Erdbeben. Euch gelüstet, fast dünkt mich's so, vergebt meinem Dünkel, ihr höheren Menschen –

– euch gelüstet nach dem schlimmsten gefährlichsten Leben, das mir am meisten Furcht macht, nach dem Leben wilder Thiere, nach Wäldern, Höhlen, steilen Bergen und Irr-Schlünden.

Und nicht die Führer aus der Gefahr gefallen euch am besten, sondern die euch von allen Wegen abführen, die Verführer. Aber, wenn solch Gelüsten an euch wirklich ist, so dünkt es mich trotzdem unmöglich.

Furcht nämlich – das ist des Menschen Erb- und Grundgefühl; aus der Furcht erklärt sich jegliches, Erbsünde und Erbtugend. Aus der Furcht wuchs auch meine Tugend, die heißt: Wissenschaft.

Die Furcht nämlich vor wildem Gethier – die wurde dem Menschen am längsten angezüchtet, einschliesslich das Thier, das er in sich selber birgt und fürchtet: – Zarathustra heißt es 'das innere Vieh'.

Solche lange alte Furcht, endlich fein geworden, geistlich, geistig – heute, dünkt mich, heißt sie: Wissenschaft." –

Also sprach der Gewissenhafte; aber Zarathustra, der eben in seine Höhle zurückkam und die letzte Rede gehört und errathen hatte, warf dem Gewissenhaften eine Hand voll Rosen zu und lachte ob seiner "Wahrheiten". "Wie! rief er, was hörte ich da eben? Wahrlich, mich dünkt, du bist ein Narr oder ich selber bin's: und deine 'Wahrheit' stelle ich rucks und flugs auf den Kopf.

Furcht nämlich – ist unsre Ausnahme. Muth aber und Abenteuer und Lust am Ungewissen, am Ungewagten, – Muth dünkt mich des Menschen ganze Vorgeschichte.

Den wildesten muthigsten Thieren hat er alle ihre Tugenden abgeneidet und abgeraubt: so erst wurde er – zum Menschen.

Dieser Muth, endlich fein geworden, geistlich, geistig, dieser Menschen-Muth mit Adler-Flügeln und Schlangen-Klugheit: der, dünkt mich, heißt heute –"

Von der Wissenschaft

"Zarathustra"! schrien Alle, die beisammen sassen, wie aus Einem Munde und machten dazu ein grosses Gelächter; es hob sich aber von ihnen wie eine schwere Wolke. Auch der Zauberer lachte und sprach mit Klugheit: "Wohlan! Er ist davon, mein böser Geist!

Und habe ich euch nicht selber vor ihm gewarnt, als ich sagte, daß er ein Betrüger sei, ein Lug- und Truggeist?

Sonderlich nämlich, wenn er sich nackend zeigt. Aber was kann ich für seine Tücken! Habe ich ihn und die Welt geschaffen?

Wohlan! Seien wir wieder gut und guter Dinge! Und ob schon Zarathustra böse blickt – seht ihn doch! er ist mir gram –:

– bevor die Nacht kommt, lernt er wieder, mich lieben und loben, er kann nicht lange leben, ohne solche Thorheiten zu thun.

Der – liebt seine Feinde: diese Kunst versteht er am besten von Allen, die ich sah. Aber er nimmt Rache dafür – an seinen Freunden!"

Also sprach der alte Zauberer, und die höheren Menschen zollten ihm Beifall: so daß Zarathustra herumgieng und mit Bosheit und Liebe seinen Freunden die Hände schüttelte, – gleichsam als Einer, der an Allen Etwas gutzumachen und abzubitten hat. Als er aber dabei an die Thür seiner Höhle kam, siehe, da gelüstete ihn schon wieder nach der guten Luft da draussen und nach seinen Thieren, – und er wollte hinaus schlüpfen.

Unter Töchtern der Wüste

1.

"Gehe nicht davon!" sagte da der Wanderer, welcher sich den Schatten Zarathustras nannte, "bleibe bei uns, es möchte uns sonst die alte dumpfe Trübsal wieder anfallen.

Schon gab uns jener alte Zauberer von seinem Schlimmsten zum Besten, und siehe doch, der gute fromme Papst da hat Thränen in den Augen und hat sich ganz wieder auf's Meer der Schwermuth eingeschifft.

Diese Könige mögen wohl vor uns noch gute Miene machen: das lernten Die nämlich von uns Allen heute am Besten! Hätten sie aber keine Zeugen, ich wette, auch bei ihnen fienge das böse Spiel wieder an –

– das böse Spiel der ziehenden Wolken, der feuchten Schwermuth, der verhängten Himmel, der gestohlenen Sonnen, der heulenden Herbst-Winde, – das böse Spiel unsres Heulens und Nothschreiens: bleibe bei uns, O Zarathustra! Hier ist viel verborgenes Elend, das reden will, viel Abend, viel Wolke, viel dumpfe Luft!

Du nährtest uns mit starker Manns-Kost und kräftigen Sprüchen: lass es nicht zu, dass uns zum Nachtisch die weichlichen weiblichen Geister wieder anfallen!

Du allein machst die Luft um dich herum stark und klar! Fand ich je auf Erden so gute Luft als bei dir in deiner Höhle?

Viele Länder sah ich doch, meine Nase lernte vielerlei Luft prüfen und abschätzen: aber bei dir schmecken meine Nüstern ihre grösste Lust!

Es sei denn, – es sei denn –, oh vergieb eine alte Erinnerung! Vergieb mir ein altes Nachtisch-Lied, das ich einst unter Töchtern der Wüste dichtete: –

– bei denen nämlich gab es gleich gute helle morgenländische Luft; dort war ich am fernsten vom wolkigen feuchten schwermüthigen Alt-Europa!

Damals liebte ich solcherlei Morgenland-Mädchen und andres blaues Himmelreich, über dem keine Wolken und keine Gedanken hängen.

Ihr glaubt es nicht, wie artig sie dasassen, wenn sie nicht tanzten, tief, aber ohne Gedanken, wie kleine Geheimnisse, wie bebänderte Räthsel, wie Nachtisch-Nüsse –

bunt und fremd fürwahr! aber ohne Wolken: Räthsel, die sich rathen lassen: solchen Mädchen zu Liebe erdachte ich damals einen Nachtisch-Psalm."

Also sprach der Wanderer und Schatten; und ehe Jemand ihm
antwortete, hatte er schon die Harfe des alten Zauberers ergriffen, die
Beine gekreuzt und blickte gelassen und weise um sich: – mit den
Nüstern aber zog er langsam und fragend die Luft ein, wie Einer, der in
neuen Ländern neue fremde Luft kostet. Darauf hob er mit einer Art
Gebrüll zu singen an.

2.

Die Wüste wächst: weh Dem, der Wüsten birgt!

– Ha! Feierlich!
In der That feierlich!
Ein würdiger Anfang!
Afrikanisch feierlich!
Eines Löwen würdig,
Oder eines moralischen Brüllaffen –
– aber Nichts für euch,
Ihr allerliebsten Freundinnen,
Zu deren Füssen mir
Zum ersten Male,
Einem Europäer, unter Palmen
Zu sitzen vergönnt ist. Sela.

Wunderbar wahrlich!
Da sitze ich nun,
Der Wüste nahe und bereits
So fern wieder der Wüste,
Auch in Nichts noch verwüstet:
Nämlich hinabgeschluckt
Von dieser kleinsten Oasis –:
– sie sperrte gerade gähnend
Ihr liebliches Maul auf,
Das wohlriechendste aller Mäulchen:
Da fiel ich hinein,
Hinab, hindurch – unter euch,
Ihr allerliebsten Freundinnen! Sela.

Heil, Heil jenem Wallfische,
Wenn er also es seinem Gaste
Wohl sein liess! – ihr versteht
Meine gelehrte Anspielung?
Heil seinem Bauche,
Wenn er also
Ein so lieblicher Oasis-Bauch war
Gleich diesem: was ich aber in Zweifel ziehe,
– dafür komme ich aus Europa,
Das zweifelsüchtiger ist als alle
Altlichen Eheweibchen.
Möge Gott es bessern!
Amen!

Da sitze ich nun,
In dieser kleinsten Oasis,
Einer Dattel gleich,
Braun, durchsüsst, goldschwürig, lüstern
Nach einem runden Mädchenmunde,
Mehr noch aber nach mädchenhaften
Eiskalten schneeweissen schneidigen
Beisszähnen: nach denen nämlich
Lechzt das Herz allen heissen Datteln. Sela.
Den genannten Südfrüchten
Ähnlich, allzuähnlich
Liege ich hier, von kleinen
Flügelkäfern
Umtänzelt und umspielt,
Insgleichen von noch kleineren
Thörichteren boshafteren
Wünschen und Einfällen,
Umlagert von euch,
Ihr stummen, ihr ahnungsvollen
Mädchen-Katzen,
Dudu und Suleika,
– umsphinxt, daß ich in Ein Wort
Viel Gefühle stopfe:
(Vergebe mir Gott
Diese Sprach-Sünde!)

– sitze hier, die beste Luft schnüffelnd,
Paradieses-Luft wahrlich,
Lichte leichte Luft, goldgestreifte,
So gute Luft nur je
Vom Monde herabfiel –
Sei es aus Zufall,
Oder geschah es aus Übermuthe?
Wie die alten Dichter erzählen.
Ich Zweifler aber ziehe es
In Zweifel, dafür aber komme ich
Aus Europa,
Das zweifelsüchtiger ist als alle
Ältlichen Eheweibchen.
Möge Gott es bessern!
Amen!

Diese schönste Luft trinkend,
Mit Nüstern geschwellt gleich Bechern,
Ohne Zukunft, ohne Erinnerungen,
So sitze ich hier, ihr
Allerliebsten Freundinnen,
Und sehe der Palme zu,
Wie sie, einer Tänzerin gleich,
Sich biegt und schmiegt und in der Hüfte wiegt,
– man thut es mit, sieht man lange zu!
Einer Tänzerin gleich, die, wie mir scheinen will,
Zu lange schon, gefährlich lange
Immer, immer nur auf Einem Beine stand?
– da vergass sie darob, wie mir scheinen will,
Das andre Bein?
Vergebens wenigstens
Suchte ich das vermißte
Zwillings-Kleinod
– nämlich das andre Bein –
In der heiligen Nähe
Ihres allerliebsten, allerzierlichsten
Fächer- und Flatter- und Flitterröckchens.

Ja, wenn ihr mir, ihr schönen Freundinnen,
Ganz glauben wollt:
Sie hat es verloren!
Es ist dahin!
Auf ewig dahin!
Das andre Bein!
Oh schade um dieses liebliche andre Bein!
Wo – mag es wohl weilen und verlassen trauern?
Das einsame Bein!
In Furcht vielleicht vor einem
Grimmen gelben blondgelockten
Löwen-Unthiere? Oder gar schon
Abgenagt, abgeknabbert –
Erbärmlich, wehe! wehe! abgeknabbert! Sela.

Oh weint mir nicht,
Weiche Herzen!
Weint mir nicht, ihr
Dattel-Herzen! Milch-Busen!
Ihr Süssholz-Herz-
Beutelchen!
Weine nicht mehr,
Bleiche Dudu!
Sei ein Mann, Suleika! Muth! Muth!
– Oder sollte vielleicht
Etwas Stärkendes, Herz-Stärkendes,
Hier am Platze sein?
Ein gesalbter Spruch?
Ein feierlicher Zuspruch? –

Ha! Herauf, Würde!
Tugend-Würde! Europäer-Würde!
Blase, blase wieder,
Blasebalg der Tugend!
Ha!
Noch einmal brüllen,
Moralisch brüllen!

Als moralischer Löwe
Vor den Töchtern der Wüste brüllen!
– Denn Tugend-Geheul,
Ihr allerliebsten Mädchen,
Ist mehr als Alles
Europäer-Inbrunst, Europäer-Heisshunger!
Und da stehe ich schon,
Als Europäer,
Ich kann nicht anders, Gott helfe mir!
Amen!

Die Wüste wächst: weh Dem, der Wüsten birgt!

Die Erweckung

1.

Nach dem Liede des Wanderers und Schattens wurde die Höhle mit Einem Male voll Lärmens und Lachens; und da die versammelten Gäste alle zugleich redeten, und auch der Esel, bei einer solchen Ermuthigung, nicht mehr still blieb, überkam Zarathustra ein kleiner Widerwille und Spott gegen seinen Besuch: ob er sich gleich ihrer Fröhlichkeit erfreute. Denn sie dünkte ihm ein Zeichen der Genesung. So schlüpfte er hinaus in's Freie und sprach zu seinen Thieren.

"Wo ist nun ihre Noth hin? sprach er, und schon athmete er selber von seinem kleinen Überdrusse auf, – bei mir verlernten sie, wie mich dünkt, das Nothschrein!

– wenn auch, leider, noch nicht das Schrein." Und Zarathustra hielt sich die Ohren zu, denn eben mischte sich das J-A des Esels wunderlich mit dem Jubel-Lärm dieser höheren Menschen.

"Sie sind lustig, begann er wieder, und wer weiss? vielleicht auf ihres Wirthes Unkosten; und lernten sie von mir lachen, so ist es doch nicht mein Lachen, das sie lernten.

Aber was liegt daran! Es sind alte Leute: sie genesen auf ihre Art, sie lachen auf ihre Art; meine Ohren haben schon Schlimmeres erduldet und wurden nicht unwirsch.

Dieser Tag ist ein Sieg: er weicht schon, er flieht, *der Geist der Schwere*, mein alter Erzfeind! Wie gut will dieser Tag enden, der so schlimm und schwer begann!

Und enden *will* er. Schon kommt der Abend: über das Meer her reitet er, der gute Reiter! Wie er sich wiegt, der Selige, Heimkehrende, in seinen purpurnen Sätteln!

Der Himmel blickt klar dazu, die Welt liegt tief: O all ihr Wunderlichen, die ihr zu mir kamt, es lohnt sich schon, bei mir zu leben!"

Also sprach Zarathustra. Und wieder kam da das Geschrei und Gelächter der höheren Menschen aus der Höhle: da begann er von Neuem.

"Sie beissen an, mein Köder wirkt, es weicht auch ihnen ihr Feind, der Geist der Schwere. Schon lernen sie über sich selber lachen: höre ich recht?

Die Erwachung

Meine Manns-Kost wirkt, mein Saft- und Kraft-Spruch: und wahrlich, ich nährte sie nicht mit Bläh-Gemüsen! Sondern mit Krieger-Kost, mit Eroberer-Kost: neue Begierden weckte ich.

Neue Hoffnungen sind in ihren Armen und Beinen, ihr Herz streckt sich aus. Sie finden neue Worte, bald wird ihr Geist Muthwillen athmen.

Solche Kost mag freilich nicht für Kinder sein, noch auch für sehnsüchtige alte und junge Weibchen. Denen überredet man anders die Eingeweide; deren Arzt und Lehrer bin ich nicht.

Der Ekel weicht diesen höheren Menschen: wohlan! das ist mein Sieg. In meinem Reiche werden sie sicher, alle dumme Scham läuft davon, sie schütten sich aus.

Sie schütten ihr Herz aus, gute Stunden kehren ihnen zurück, sie feiern und käuen wieder, – sie werden dankbar.

Das nehme ich als das beste Zeichen: sie werden dankbar. Nicht lange noch, und sie denken sich Feste aus und stellen Denksteine ihren alten Freuden auf.

Es sind Genesende!" Also sprach Zarathustra fröhlich zu seinem Herzen und schaute hinaus; seine Thiere aber drängten sich an ihn und ehrten sein Glück und sein Stillschweigen.

2.

Plötzlich aber erschrak das Ohr Zarathustras: die Höhle nämlich, welche bisher voller Lärmens und Gelächters war, wurde mit Einem Male todtenstill; – seine Nase aber roch einen wohlriechenden Qualm und Weihrauch, wie von brennenden Pinien-Zapfen.

"Was geschieht? Was treiben sie?" fragte er sich und schlich zum Eingange heran, dass er seinen Gästen, unvermerkt, zusehn könne. Aber, Wunder über Wunder! was musste er da mit seinen eignen Augen sehn!

"Sie sind Alle wieder fromm geworden, sie beten, sie sind toll!" – sprach er und verwunderte sich über die Maassen. Und, fürwahr!, alle diese höheren Menschen, die zwei Könige, der Papst ausser Dienst, der schlimme Zauberer, der freiwillige Bettler, der Wanderer und Schatten, der alte Wahrsager, der Gewissenhafte des Geistes und der hässlichste Mensch: sie lagen Alle gleich Kindern und gläubigen alten Weibchen auf den Knien und beteten den Esel an. Und eben begann der hässlichste Mensch zu gurgeln und zu schnauben, wie als ob etwas Unaussprechliches aus ihm heraus wolle; als er es aber wirklich bis zu Worten gebracht hatte, siehe, da war es eine fromme seltsame Litanei zur

Lobpreisung des angebeteten und angeräucherten Esels. Diese Litanei aber klang also:
Amen! Und Lob und Ehre und Weisheit und Dank und Preis und Stärke sei unserm Gott, von Ewigkeit zu Ewigkeit!
– Der Esel aber schrie dazu J=A.
Er trägt unsre Last, er nahm Knechtsgestalt an, er ist geduldsam von Herzen und redet niemals Nein; und wer seinen Gott liebt, der züchtigt ihn.
– Der Esel aber schrie dazu J=A.
Er redet nicht: es sei denn, daß er zur Welt, die er Schuf, immer Ja sagt: also preist er seine Welt. Seine Schlauheit ist es, die nicht redet: so bekommt er selten Unrecht.
– Der Esel aber schrie dazu J=A.
Unscheinbar geht er durch die Welt. Grau ist die Leib=Farbe, in welche er seine Tugend hüllt. Hat er Geist, so verbirgt er ihn; Jedermann aber glaubt an seine langen Ohren.
– Der Esel aber schrie dazu J=A.
Welche verborgene Weisheit ist das, daß er lange Ohren trägt und allein ja und nimmer Nein sagt! Hat er nicht die Welt erschaffen nach seinem Bilde, nämlich so dumm als möglich?
– Der Esel aber schrie dazu J=A.
Du gehst gerade und krumme Wege; es kümmert dich wenig, was uns Menschen gerade oder krumm dünkt. Jenseits von Gut und Böse ist dein Reich. Es ist deine Unschuld, nicht zu wissen, was Unschuld ist.
– Der Esel aber schrie dazu J=A.
Siehe doch, wie du Niemanden von dir stössest, die Bettler nicht, noch die Könige. Die Kindlein lässest du zu dir kommen, und wenn dich die bösen Buben locken, so sprichst du einfältiglich J=A.
– Der Esel aber schrie dazu J=A.
Du liebst Eselinnen und frische Feigen, du bist kein Kostverächter. Eine Distel kitzelt dir das Herz, wenn du gerade Hunger hast. Darin liegt eines Gottes Weisheit.
– Der Esel aber schrie dazu J=A.

Das Eselsfest

1.

An dieser Stelle der Litanei aber konnte Zarathustra sich nicht länger bemeistern, schrie selber J-A, lauter noch als der Esel, und sprang mitten unter seine tollgewordenen Gäste. "Aber was treibt ihr da, ihr Menschenkinder? rief er, indem er die Betenden vom Boden empor riss. Wehe, wenn auch Jemand Anderes zusähe als Zarathustra:

Jeder würde urtheilen, ihr wäret mit eurem neuen Glauben die ärgsten Gotteslästerer oder die thörichtsten aller alten Weiblein!

Und du selber, du alter Papst, wie stimmt Das mit dir selber zusammen, daß du solchergestalt einen Esel hier als Gott anbetest?" –

"O Zarathustra, antwortete der Papst, vergieb mir, aber in Dingen Gottes bin ich aufgeklärter noch als du. Und so ist's billig.

Lieber Gott also anbeten, in dieser Gestalt, als in gar keiner Gestalt! Denke über diesen Spruch nach, mein hoher Freund: du erräthst geschwind, in solchem Spruch steckt Weisheit.

Der, welcher sprach 'Gott ist ein Geist' – der machte bisher auf Erden den grössten Schritt und Sprung zum Unglauben: solch Wort ist auf Erden nicht leicht wieder gut zu machen!

Mein altes Herz springt und hüpft darob, daß es auf Erden noch Etwas anzubeten giebt. Vergieb das, O Zarathustra, einem alten frommen Papst-Herzen!" –

– "Und du, sagte Zarathustra zu dem Wanderer und Schatten, du nennst und wähnst dich einen freien Geist? Und treibst hier solchen Götzen- und Pfaffendienst?

Schlimmer, wahrlich, treibst du's hier noch als bei deinen schlimmen braunen Mädchen, du schlimmer neuer Gläubiger!"

"Schlimm genug, antwortete der Wanderer und Schatten, du hast Recht: aber was kann ich dafür! Der alte Gott lebt wieder, O Zarathustra, du magst reden, was du willst.

Der hässlichste Mensch ist an Allem schuld: der hat ihn wieder aufgeweckt. Und wenn er sagt, daß er ihn einst getödtet habe: Tod ist bei Göttern immer nur ein Vorurtheil."

– Und du, sprach Zarathustra, du schlimmer alter Zauberer, was thatest du! Wer soll, in dieser freien Zeit, fürderhin an dich glauben, wenn du an solche Götter-Eselelen glaubst?

Es war eine Dummheit, was du thatest; wie konntest du, du Kluger, eine solche Dummheit thun!

"O Zarathustra, antwortete der kluge Zauberer, du hast Recht, es war eine Dummheit, – es ist mir auch schwer genug geworden."

– Und du gar, sagte Zarathustra, zu dem Gewissenhaften des Geistes, erwäge doch und lege den Finger an deine Nase! Geht hier denn Nichts wider dein Gewissen? ist dein Geist nicht zu reinlich für dies Beten und den Dunst dieser Betbrüder?"

"Es ist Etwas daran, antwortete der Gewissenhafte und legte den Finger an die Nase, es ist Etwas an diesem Schauspiele, das meinem Gewissen sogar wohlthut.

Vielleicht, daß ich an Gott nicht glauben darf: gewiss aber ist, daß Gott mir in dieser Gestalt noch am glaubwürdigsten dünkt.

Gott soll ewig sein, nach dem Zeugnisse der Frömmsten: wer so viel Zeit hat, lässt sich Zeit. So langsam und so dumm als möglich: damit kann ein Solcher es doch sehr weit bringen.

Und wer des Geistes zu viel hat, der möchte sich wohl in die Dumm- und Narrheit selber vernarren. Denke über dich selber nach, O Zarathustra!

Du selber – wahrlich! auch du könntest wohl aus Überfluss und Weisheit zu einem Esel werden.

Geht nicht ein vollkommner Weiser gern auf den krümmsten Wegen? Der Augenschein lehrt es, O Zarathustra, – dein Augenschein!"

– "Und du selber zuletzt, sprach Zarathustra und wandte sich gegen den hässlichsten Menschen, der immer noch auf dem Boden lag, den Arm zu dem Esel emporhebend (er gab ihm nämlich Wein zu trinken). Sprich, du Unaussprechlicher, was hast du da gemacht!

Du dünkst mich verwandelt, dein Auge glüht, der Mantel des Erhabenen liegt um deine Hässlichkeit: was thatest du?

Ist es denn wahr, was jene sagen, daß du ihn wieder aufewecktest? Und wozu? War er nicht mit Grund abgetödtet und abgethan?

Du selber dünkst mich aufgeweckt: was thatest du? was kehrtest du um? Was bekehrtest du dich? Sprich, du Unaussprechlicher!"

"O Zarathustra, antwortete der hässlichste Mensch, du bist ein Schelm!
Ob Der noch lebt oder wieder lebt oder gründlich todt ist, – wer von uns Beiden weiss Das am Besten? Ich frage dich.
Eins aber weiss ich, – von dir selber lernte ich's einst, O Zarathustra: wer am gründlichsten tödten will, der lacht.
'Nicht durch Zorn, sondern durch Lachen tödtet man' – so sprachst du einst. O Zarathustra, du Verborgener, du Vernichter ohne Zorn, du gefährlicher Heiliger, – du bist ein Schelm!"

2.

Da aber geschah es, daß Zarathustra, verwundert über lauter solche Schelmen-Antworten, zur Thür seiner Höhle zurück sprang und, gegen alle seine Gäste gewandet, mit starker Stimme schrie:
"O ihr Schalks-Narren allesammt, ihr Possenreisser! Was verstellt und versteckt ihr euch vor mir!

Wie doch einem jeden von euch das Herz zappelte vor Lust und Bosheit, darob, daß ihr endlich einmal wieder wurdet wie die Kindlein, nämlich fromm, –

– daß ihr endlich wieder thatet wie Kinder thun, nämlich betetet, hände-faltetet und 'lieber Gott' sagtet!

Aber nun lasst mir diese Kinderstube, meine eigne Höhle, wo heute alle Kinderei zu Hause ist. Kühlt hier draussen euren heissen Kinder-Übermuth und Herzenslärm ab!

Freilich: so ihr nicht werdet wie die Kindlein, so kommt ihr nicht in das Himmelreich. (Und Zarathustra zeigte mit den Händen nach Oben.)

Aber wir wollen auch gar nicht in's Himmelreich: Männer sind wir worden, – so wollen wir das Erdenreich."

3.

Und noch einmal hob Zarathustra an zu reden. "O meine neuen Freunde, sprach er, – ihr Wunderlichen, ihr höheren Menschen, wie gut gefallt ihr mir nun, –

– seit ihr wieder fröhlich wurdet! Ihr seid wahrlich Alle aufgeblüht: mich dünkt, solchen Blumen, wie ihr seid, thun neue Feste noth,

– ein kleiner tapferer Unsinn, irgend ein Gottesdienst und Eselsfest, irgend ein alter fröhlicher Zarathustra-Narr, ein Brausewind, der auch die Seelen hell bläst.

Vergesst die Nacht und dies Eselsfest nicht, ihr höheren Menschen! Das erfandet ihr bei mir, Das nehme ich als gutes Wahrzeichen, – Solcherlei erfinden nur Genesende!

Und feiert ihr es abermals, dieses Eselsfest, thut's euch zu Liebe, thut's auch mir zu Liebe! Und zu meinem Gedächtniss!"

Also sprach Zarathustra.

Das Nachtwandler=Lied

1.

Inzwischen aber war Einer nach dem Andern hinaus getreten, in's Freie und in die kühle nachdenkliche Nacht; Zarathustra selber aber führte den hässlichsten Menschen an der Hand, daß er ihm seine Nacht=Welt und den grossen runden Mond und die silbernen Wasserstürze bei seiner Höhle zeige. Da standen sie endlich still bei einander, lauter alte Leute, aber mit einem getrösteten tapferen Herzen und verwundert bei sich, daß es ihnen auf Erden so wohl war; die Heimlichkeit der Nacht aber kam ihnen näher und näher an's Herz. Und von Neuem dachte Zarathustra bei sich: "oh wie gut sie mir nun gefallen, diese höheren Menschen!" – aber er sprach es nicht aus, denn er ehrte ihr Glück und ihr Stillschweigen. –

Da aber geschah Das, was an jenem erstaunlichen langen Tage das Erstaunlichste war: der hässlichste Mensch begann noch einmal und zum letzten Mal zu gurgeln und zu schnauben, und als er es bis zu Worten gebracht hatte, siehe, da sprang eine Frage rund und reinlich aus seinem Munde, eine gute tiefe klare Frage, welche Allen, die ihm zuhörten, das Herz im Leibe bewegte.

"Meine Freunde insgesammt, sprach der hässlichste Mensch, was dünket euch? Um dieses Tags Willen – ich bin's zum ersten Male zufrieden, daß ich das ganze Leben lebte.

Und daß ich so viel bezeuge, ist mir noch nicht genug. Es lohnt sich auf der Erde zu leben: Ein Tag, Ein Fest mit Zarathustra lehrte mich die Erde lieben.

'War Das – das Leben?' will ich zum Tode sprechen. 'Wohlan! Noch einmal!'

Meine Freunde, was dünket euch? Wollt ihr nicht gleich mir zum Tode sprechen: War Das – das Leben? Um Zarathustras Willen, wohlan! Noch einmal!" – –

Also sprach der hässlichste Mensch; es war aber nicht lange vor Mitternacht. Und was glaubt ihr wohl, daß damals sich zutrug? Sobald die höheren Menschen seine Frage hörten, wurden sie sich mit Einem Male ihrer Verwandlung und Genesung bewusst, und wer ihnen dieselbe gegeben habe: da sprangen sie auf Zarathustra zu, dankend, verehrend, liebkosend, ihm die Hände küssend, so wie es der Art eines Jeden eigen war: also daß Einige lachten, Einige weinten. Der alte

Wahrsager aber tanzte vor Vergnügen; und wenn er auch, wie manche Erzähler meinen, damals voll süssen Weines war, so war er gewisslich noch voller des süssen Lebens und hatte aller Müdigkeit abgesagt. Es giebt sogar Solche, die erzählen, daß damals der Esel getanzt habe: nicht umsonst nämlich habe ihm der hässlichste Mensch vorher Wein zu trinken gegeben. Dies mag sich nun so verhalten oder auch anders; und wenn in Wahrheit an jenem Abende der Esel nicht getanzt hat, so geschahen doch damals grössere und seltsamere Wunderdinge als es das Tanzen eines Esels wäre. Kurz, wie das Sprichwort Zarathustras lautet: "was liegt daran!"

2.

Zarathustra aber, als sich dies mit dem hässlichsten Menschen zutrug, stand da, wie ein Trunkener: sein Blick erlosch, seine Zunge lallte, seine Füsse schwankten. Und wer möchte auch errathen, welche Gedanken dabei über Zarathustras Seele liefen? Ersichtlich aber wich sein Geist zurück und floh voraus und war in weiten Fernen und gleichsam "auf hohem Joche, wie geschrieben steht, zwischen zwei Meeren,
— zwischen Vergangenem und Zukünftigem als schwere Wolke wandelnd." Allgemach aber, während ihn die höheren Menschen in den Armen hielten, kam er ein Wenig zu sich selber zurück und wehrte mit den Händen dem Gedränge der Verehrenden und Besorgten; doch sprach er nicht. Mit Einem Male aber wandte er schnell den Kopf, denn er schien Etwas zu hören: da legte er den Finger an den Mund und sprach: "Kommt!"

Und alsbald wurde es rings still und heimlich; aus der Tiefe aber kam langsam der Klang einer Glocke herauf. Zarathustra horchte darnach, gleich den höheren Menschen; dann aber legte er zum andern Male den Finger an den Mund und sprach wiederum: "Kommt! Kommt! Es geht gen Mitternacht!" — und seine Stimme hatte sich verwandelt. Aber immer noch rührte er sich nicht von der Stelle: da wurde es noch stiller und heimlicher, und Alles horchte, auch der Esel, und Zarathustras Ehrenthiere, der Adler und die Schlange, insgleichen die Höhle Zarathustras und der grosse kühle Mond und die Nacht selber. Zarathustra aber legte zum dritten Male die Hand an den Mund und sprach:

Kommt! Kommt! Kommt! Lasst uns jetzo wandeln! Es ist die Stunde: lasst uns in die Nacht wandeln!

Das Nachtwandler-Lied

3.

Ihr höheren Menschen, es geht gen Mitternacht: da will ich euch Etwas in die Ohren sagen, wie jene alte Glocke es mir in's Ohr sagt, –
– so heimlich, so schrecklich, so herzlich, wie jene Mitternachts-Glocke zu mir es redet, die mehr erlebt hat als Ein Mensch:
– welche schon eurer Väter Herzens-Schmerzens-Schläge abzählte –
ach! ach! wie sie seufzt! wie sie im Traume lacht! die alte tiefe tiefe Mitternacht!
Still! Still! Da hört sich Manches, das am Tage nicht laut werden darf; nun aber, bei kühler Luft, da auch aller Lärm eurer Herzen stille ward, –
– nun redet es, nun hört es sich, nun schleicht es sich in nächtliche überwache Seelen: ach! ach! wie sie seufzt! wie sie im Traume lacht!
– hörst du's nicht, wie sie heimlich, schrecklich, herzlich zu dir redet, die alte tiefe tiefe Mitternacht?
O Mensch, gieb Acht!

4.

Wehe mir! Wo ist die Zeit hin? Sank ich nicht in tiefe Brunnen? Die Welt schläft –
Ach! Ach! Der Hund heult, der Mond scheint. Lieber will ich sterben, sterben, als euch sagen, was mein Mitternachts-Herz eben denkt.
Nun starb ich schon. Es ist dahin. Spinne, was spinnst du um mich? Willst du Blut? Ach! Ach! der Thau fällt, die Stunde kommt –
– die Stunde, wo mich fröstelt und friert, die fragt und fragt und fragt: "wer hat Herz genug dazu?
– wer soll der Erde Herr sein? Wer will sagen: so sollt ihr laufen, ihr grossen und kleinen Ströme!"
– die Stunde naht: O Mensch, du höherer Mensch, gieb Acht! diese Rede ist für feine Ohren, für deine Ohren *was spricht die tiefe Mitternacht?*

5.

Es trägt mich dahin, meine Seele tanzt. Tagewerk! Tagewerk! Wer soll der Erde Herr sein?
Der Mond ist kühl, der Wind schweigt. Ach! Ach! flogt ihr schon hoch genug? Ihr tanztet: aber ein Bein ist doch kein Flügel.

Ihr guten Tänzer, nun ist alle Lust vorbei, Wein ward Hefe, jeder Becher ward mürbe, die Gräber stammeln.

Ihr flogt nicht hoch genug: nun stammeln die Gräber "erlöst doch die Todten! Warum ist so lange Nacht? Macht uns nicht der Mond trunken?"

Ihr höheren Menschen, erlöst doch die Gräber, weckt die Leichname auf! Ach, was gräbt noch der Wurm? Es naht, es naht die Stunde, -

- es brummt die Glocke, es schnarrt noch das Herz, es gräbt noch der Holzwurm, der Herzenswurm. Ach! Ach! Die Welt ist tief!

6.

Süsse Leier! Süsse Leier! Ich liebe deinen Ton, deinen trunkenen Unken-Ton! - wie lang her, wie fern her kommt mir dein Ton, weit her, von den Teichen der Liebe!

Du alte Glocke, du süsse Leier! Jeder Schmerz riss dir in's Herz, Vaterschmerz, Väterschmerz, Urväterschmerz, deine Rede wurde reif,-

- reif gleich goldnem Herbste und Nachmittage, gleich meinem Einsiedlerherzen - nun redest du: die Welt selber ward reif, die Traube bräunt,

- nun will sie sterben, vor Glück sterben. Ihr höheren Menschen, riecht ihr's nicht? Es quillt heimlich ein Geruch herauf,

- ein Duft und Geruch der Ewigkeit, ein rosenseliger, brauner Gold-Wein-Geruch von altem Glücke,

- von trunkenem Mitternachts-Sterbeglücke, welches singt: die Welt ist tief, und tiefer als der Tag gedacht!

7.

Lass mich! Lass mich! Ich bin zu rein für dich. Rühre mich nicht an! Ward meine Welt nicht eben vollkommen?

Meine Haut ist zu rein für deine Hände. Lass mich, du dummer tölpischer dumpfer Tag! ist die Mitternacht nicht heller?

Die Reinsten sollen der Erde Herrn sein, die Unerkanntesten, Stärksten, die Mitternachts-Seelen, die heller und tiefer sind als jeder Tag.

O Tag, du tappst nach mir? Du tastest nach meinem Glücke? Ich bin dir reich, einsam, eine Schatzgrube, eine Goldkammer?

O Welt, du willst mich? Bin ich dir weltlich? Bin ich dir geistlich? Bin ich dir göttlich? Aber Tag und Welt, ihr seid zu plump, -

– habt klügere Hände, greift nach tieferem Glücke, nach tieferem Unglücke, greift nach irgend einem Gotte, greift nicht nach mir:
– mein Unglück, mein Glück ist tief, du wunderlicher Tag, aber doch bin ich kein Gott, keine Gottes-Hölle: tief ist ihr Weh.

8.

Gottes Weh ist tiefer, du wunderliche Welt! Greife nach Gottes Weh, nicht nach mir! Was bin ich! Eine trunkene süsse Leier, –
– eine Mitternachts-Leier, eine Glocken-Unke, die Niemand versteht, aber welche reden muss, vor Tauben, ihr höheren Menschen! Denn ihr versteht mich nicht!
Dahin! Dahin! O Jugend! O Mittag! O Nachmittag! Nun kam Abend und Nacht und Mitternacht, – der Hund heult, der Wind:
– ist der Wind nicht ein Hund? Er winselt, er kläfft, er heult. Ach! Ach! wie sie seufzt! wie sie lacht, wie sie röchelt und keucht, die Mitternacht!
Wie sie eben nüchtern spricht, diese trunkene Dichterin! sie übertrat wohl ihre Trunkenheit? sie wurde überwach? sie käut zurück?
– ihr Weh käut sie zurück, im Traume, die alte tiefe Mitternacht, und mehr noch ihre Lust. Lust nämlich, wenn schon Weh tief ist:
Lust ist tiefer noch als Herzeleid.

9.

Du Weinstock! Was preisest du mich? Ich schnitt dich doch! Ich bin grausam, du blutest –: was will dein Lob meiner trunkenen Grausamkeit?
"Was vollkommen ward, alles Reife – will sterben!" so redest du. Gesegnet, gesegnet sei das Winzermesser! Aber alles Unreife will leben: wehe!
Weh spricht: "Vergeh! Weg, du Wehe!" Aber Alles, was leidet, will leben, dass es reif werde und lustig und sehnsüchtig,
– sehnsüchtig nach Fernerem, Höherem, Hellerem. "Ich will Erben, so spricht Alles, was leidet, ich will Kinder, ich will nicht mich," –
Lust aber will nicht Erben, nicht Kinder, – Lust will sich selber, will Ewigkeit, will Wiederkunft, will Alles-sich-ewig-gleich.
Weh spricht: "Brich, blute, Herz! Wandle, Bein! Flügel, flieg! Hinan! Hinauf! Schmerz!" Wohlan! Wohlauf! O mein altes Herz: Weh spricht: "vergeh!"

10.

Ihr höheren Menschen, was dünket euch? Bin ich ein Wahrsager? Ein Träumender? Trunkener? Ein Traumdeuter? Eine Mitternachts-Glocke?
Ein Tropfen Thaus? Ein Dunst und Duft der Ewigkeit? Hört ihr's nicht? Riecht ihr's nicht? Eben ward meine Welt vollkommen, Mitternacht ist auch Mittag, –
Schmerz ist auch eine Lust, Fluch ist auch ein Segen, Nacht ist auch eine Sonne, – geht davon oder ihr lernt: ein Weiser ist auch ein Narr.
Sagtet ihr jemals ja zu Einer Lust? O, meine Freunde, so sagtet ihr Ja auch zu allem Wehe. Alle Dinge sind verkettet, verfädelt, verliebt, –
– wolltet ihr jemals Ein Mal zweimal, spracht ihr jemals "du gefällst mir, Glück! Husch! Augenblick!" so wolltet ihr Alles zurück!
– Alles von neuem, Alles ewig, Alles verkettet, verfädelt, verliebt, oh so liebtet ihr die Welt, –
– ihr Ewigen, liebt sie ewig und allezeit: und auch zum Weh sprecht ihr: vergeh, aber komm zurück! Denn alle Lust will – Ewigkeit!

11.

Alle Lust will aller Dinge Ewigkeit, will Honig, will Hefe, will trunkene Mitternacht, will Gräber, will Gräber-Thränen-Trost, will vergüldetes Abendroth –
– was will nicht Lust! sie ist durstiger, herzlicher, hungriger, schrecklicher, heimlicher als alles Weh, sie will sich, sie beißt in sich, des Ringes Wille ringt in ihr, –
– sie will Liebe, sie will Hass, sie ist überreich, schenkt, wirft weg, bettelt, daß Einer sie nimmt, dankt dem Nehmenden, sie möchte gern gehasst sein, –
– so reich ist Lust, daß sie nach Wehe durstet, nach Hölle, nach Hass, nach Schmach, nach dem Krüppel, nach Welt, – denn diese Welt, oh ihr kennt sie ja!
Ihr höheren Menschen, nach euch sehnt sie sich, die Lust, die unbändige, selige, – nach eurem Weh, ihr Mißrathenen! Nach Mißrathenem sehnt sich alle ewige Lust.
Denn alle Lust will sich selber, drum will sie auch Herzeleid! Oh Glück, oh Schmerz! Oh brich, Herz! Ihr höheren Menschen, lernt es doch, Lust will Ewigkeit,
– Lust will aller Dinge Ewigkeit, will tiefe, tiefe Ewigkeit!

Das Nachtwandler-Lied

12.

Lerntet ihr nun mein Lied? Erriethet ihr, was es will? Wohlan! Wohlauf! Ihr höheren Menschen, so singt mir nun meinen Rundgesang!

Singt mir nun selber das Lied, dess Name ist "Noch einmal", dess Sinn ist "in alle Ewigkeit!", singt, ihr höheren Menschen, Zarathustras Rundgesang!

O Mensch! Gieb Acht!
Was spricht die tiefe Mitternacht?
"Ich schlief, ich schlief —,
Aus tiefem Traum bin ich erwacht: —
Die Welt ist tief,
Und tiefer als der Tag gedacht.
Tief ist ihr Weh —,
Lust — tiefer noch als Herzeleid:
Weh spricht: Vergeh!
Doch alle Lust will Ewigkeit
will tiefe, tiefe Ewigkeit!"

Das Zeichen

Des Morgens aber nach dieser Nacht sprang Zarathustra von seinem Lager auf, gürtete sich die Lenden und kam heraus aus seiner Höhle, glühend und stark, wie eine Morgensonne, die aus dunklen Bergen kommt.

"Du grosses Gestirn, sprach er, wie er einstmal gesprochen hatte, du tiefes Glücks-Auge, was wäre all dein Glück, wenn du nicht Die hättest, welchen du leuchtest!

Und wenn sie in ihren Kammern blieben, während du schon wach bist und kommst und schenkst und austheilst: wie würde darob deine stolze Scham zürnen!

Wohlan! sie schlafen noch, diese höheren Menschen, während ich wach bin: das sind nicht meine rechten Gefährten! Nicht auf sie warte ich hier in meinen Bergen.

Zu meinem Werke will ich, zu meinem Tage: aber sie verstehen nicht, was die Zeichen meines Morgens sind, mein Schritt – ist für sie kein Weckruf.

Sie schlafen noch in meiner Höhle, ihr Traum käut noch an meinen Mitternächten. Das Ohr, das nach mir horcht, – das gehorchende Ohr fehlt in ihren Gliedern."

– Dies hatte Zarathustra zu seinem Herzen gesprochen, als die Sonne aufgieng: da blickte er fragend in die Höhe, denn er hörte über sich den scharfen Ruf seines Adlers. "Wohlan! rief er hinauf, so gefällt und gebührt es mir. Meine Thiere sind wach, denn ich bin wach.

Mein Adler ist wach und ehrt gleich mir die Sonne. Mit Adlers-Klauen greift er nach dem neuen Lichte. Ihr seid meine rechten Thiere; ich liebe euch.

Aber noch fehlen mir meine rechten Menschen!" –

Also sprach Zarathustra; da aber geschah es, dass er sich plötzlich wie von unzähligen Vögeln umschwärmt und umflattert hörte, – das Geschwirr so vieler Flügel aber und das Gedräng um sein Haupt war so gross, dass er die Augen schloss. Und wahrlich, einer Wolke gleich fiel es über ihn her, einer Wolke von Pfeilen gleich, welche sich über einen neuen Feind ausschüttet. Aber siehe, hier war es eine Wolke der Liebe, und über einen neuen Freund.

"Was geschieht mir?" dachte Zarathustra in seinem erstaunten Herzen und liess sich langsam auf dem grossen Steine nieder, der neben dem

Das Zeichen

Ausgange seiner Höhle lag. Aber, indem er mit den Händen um sich und über sich und unter sich griff, und den zärtlichen Vögeln wehrte, siehe, da geschah ihm etwas noch Seltsameres: er griff nämlich dabei unvermerkt in ein dichtes warmes Haar-Gezottel hinein; zugleich aber erscholl vor ihm ein Gebrüll, – ein sanftes langes Löwen-Brüllen.

"Das Zeichen kommt," sprach Zarathustra und sein Herz verwandelte sich. Und in Wahrheit, als es helle vor ihm wurde, da lag ihm ein gelbes mächtiges Gethier zu Füssen und schmiegte das Haupt an seine Knie und wollte nicht von ihm lassen vor Liebe und that einem Hunde gleich, welcher seinen alten Herrn wiederfindet. Die Tauben aber waren mit ihrer Liebe nicht minder eifrig als der Löwe; und jedes Mal, wenn eine Taube über die Nase des Löwen huschte, schüttelte der Löwe das Haupt und wunderte sich und lachte dazu.

Zu dem Allen sprach Zarathustra nur Ein Wort: "meine Kinder sind nahe, meine Kinder" –, dann wurde er ganz stumm. Sein Herz aber war gelöst, und aus seinen Augen tropften Thränen herab und fielen auf seine Hände. Und er achtete keines Dings mehr und sass da, unbeweglich und ohne daß er sich noch gegen die Thiere wehrte. Da flogen die Tauben ab und zu und setzten sich ihm auf die Schulter und liebkosten sein weisses Haar und wurden nicht müde mit Zärtlichkeit und Frohlocken. Der starke Löwe aber leckte immer die Thränen, welche auf die Hände Zarathustras herabfielen und brüllte und brummte schüchtern dazu. Also trieben es diese Thiere. –

Dies Alles dauerte eine lange Zeit, oder eine kurze Zeit: denn, recht gesprochen, giebt es für dergleichen Dinge auf Erden keine Zeit –. Inzwischen aber waren die höheren Menschen in der Höhle Zarathustras wach geworden und ordneten sich mit einander zu einem Zuge an, daß sie Zarathustra entgegen giengen und ihm den Morgengruss böten: denn sie hatten gefunden, als sie erwachten, daß er schon nicht mehr unter ihnen weilte. Als sie aber zur Thür der Höhle gelangten, und das Geräusch ihrer Schritte ihnen voranlief, da stutzte der Löwe gewaltig, kehrte sich mit Einem Male von Zarathustra ab und sprang, wild brüllend, auf die Höhle los; die höheren Menschen aber, als sie ihn brüllen hörten, schrien alle auf, wie mit Einem Munde, und flohen zurück und waren im Nu verschwunden.

Zarathustra selber aber, betäubt und fremd, erhob sich von seinem Sitz, sah um sich, stand staunend da, fragte sein Herz, besann sich und war allein. "Was hörte ich doch? sprach er endlich langsam, was geschah mir eben?"

Und schon kam ihm die Erinnerung, und er begriff mit Einem Blicke Alles, was zwischen Gestern und Heute sich begeben hatte. "Hier ist ja der Stein, sprach er und strich sich den Bart, auf Dem sass ich gestern am Morgen; und hier trat der Wahrsager zu mir, und hier hörte ich zuerst den Schrei, den ich eben hörte, den grossen Nothschrei.

O ihr höheren Menschen, von eurer Noth war's ja, dass gestern am Morgen jener alte Wahrsager mir wahrsagte, –

– zu eurer Noth wollte er mich verführen und versuchen: O Zarathustra, sprach er zu mir, ich komme, dass ich dich zu deiner letzten Sünde verführe.

Zu meiner letzten Sünde? rief Zarathustra und lachte zornig über sein eigenes Wort: was blieb mir doch aufgespart als meine letzte Sünde?"

– Und noch einmal versank Zarathustra in sich und setzte sich wieder auf den grossen Stein nieder und sann nach. Plötzlich sprang er empor, –

"Mitleiden! Das Mitleiden mit dem höheren Menschen! schrie er auf, und sein Antlitz verwandelte sich in Erz. Wohlan! Das – hatte seine Zeit!

Mein Leid und mein Mitleiden – was liegt daran! Trachte ich denn nach Glücke? Ich trachte nach meinem Werke!

Wohlan! Der Löwe kam, meine Kinder sind nahe, Zarathustra ward reif, meine Stunde kam: –

Dies ist mein Morgen, mein Tag hebt an: herauf nun, herauf, du grosser Mittag!" – –

Also sprach Zarathustra und verliess seine Höhle, glühend und stark, wie eine Morgensonne, die aus dunklen Bergen kommt.

War's nicht für euch,
daß sich des Gletschers Grau
Heut schmückt mit Rosen?
Euch sucht der Bach,
sehnsüchtig drängen, stossen
Sich Wind und Wolke höher heut in's Blau,
Nach euch zu spähn
aus fernster Vogel=Schau.

∞

Die letzte Versuchung Zarathustras

von

FRIEDRICH NIETZSCHE

Inhalt

Also Sprach Zarathustra 97
Das Honig-Opfer 101
Der Nothschrei 105
Gespräch mit den Königen 108
Der Blutegel 112
Der Zauberer 115
Ausser Dienst 122
Der häßlichste Mensch 126
Der freiwillige Bettler 131
Der Schatten 135
Mittags 138
Die Begrüssung 141
Das Abendmahl 146
Vom höheren Menschen 148
Von der Wissenschaft 163
Unter Töchtern der Wüste 166
Die Erweckung 172
Das Eselsfest 175
Das Nachtwandler-Lied 179
Das Zeichen 186

*Other bilingual classics
in this series:*

Aristophanes BIRDS

Aristophanes PEACE

Aristophanes ARMYSUNDUA

QUIDZUNC

www.ingramcontent.com/pod-product-compliance
Lightning Source LLC
Chambersburg PA
CBHW051945290426
44110CB00015B/2110